RESTful API Design

APIs your consumers will love

Matthias Biehl

RESTful API Design
Copyright © 2016 by Matthias Biehl
All rights reserved, including the right to reproduce
this book or portions thereof in any form whatsoever.

First edition: August 2016

Biehl, Matthias
    API-University Press
    Volume 3 of the API-University Series.
    Includes illustrations, bibliographical references and index.
    ISBN-13: 978-1514735169
    ISBN-10: 1514735164

API-University Press
http://www.api-university.com
info@api-university.com

Contents

1. **Introduction**   **17**
   - 1.1. What is an API? 17
   - 1.2. Why APIs? 18
   - 1.3. How are APIs used? 20
   - 1.4. What is API Design? 21
   - 1.5. What is the difference between API Design and API Architecture? 22
   - 1.6. Why is API Design important? 24
   - 1.7. Why should I build RESTful APIs? 25
   - 1.8. Why do I need OpenAPI, Swagger or RAML? . . 26
   - 1.9. How to put API Design into Practice? 27

2. **Consumer-Oriented API Design: APIs as Products**   **29**
   - 2.1. APIs are Products 29
   - 2.2. API Consumers 30
   - 2.3. Consumer-Oriented APIs 31
   - 2.4. Building Consumer-Oriented APIs 32
     - 2.4.1. Identify the Prototypical API Consumers   32
     - 2.4.2. Engage with API Consumers 33
     - 2.4.3. Learn about the Solution Architecture of Consumers 33
   - 2.5. Summary 34

3. **API Design and Development Approach**   **35**
   - 3.1. Foundations 35
     - 3.1.1. Consumer-Oriented Design Approach . . 36
       - 3.1.1.1. Inside-out Approach 36

		3.1.1.2. Outside-in Approach	36
	3.1.2.	Contract-First Design Approach	37
	3.1.3.	Agile Design Approach	38
	3.1.4.	Simulation-based Design	38
		3.1.4.1. Simulation of Backends	39
		3.1.4.2. Simulation of the API	40
	3.1.5.	Conclusion	40
3.2.	Design Approach		41
	3.2.1.	Overview	41
	3.2.2.	Phase 1: Domain Analysis	42
		3.2.2.1. Verification of Phase 1: Simulation & Demo App	44
	3.2.3.	Phase 2: Architectural and Frontend Design	45
		3.2.3.1. Verification of Phase 2: Simulation & Demo App	46
	3.2.4.	Phase 3: Prototyping	47
		3.2.4.1. Validation of Phase 3: Acceptance Tests with Pilot Consumers	49
	3.2.5.	Phase 4: Implementation for Production .	50
		3.2.5.1. Verification of Phase 4: Acceptance Tests with Pilot Consumers	51
	3.2.6.	Phase 5: Publish	51
		3.2.6.1. Verification of Phase 5: Study Metrics, Reports and Logs . . .	52
	3.2.7.	Phase 6: Maintenance	54
3.3.	Discussion		55
	3.3.1.	Hand-over Points	55
	3.3.2.	Pre-Work vs. Actual Work	55
3.4.	Summary		56

4. API Design with API Description Languages — **57**
4.1. What are API Description Languages? 57
4.2. Usage 58
    4.2.1. Communication and Documentation . . . 59

		4.2.2.	Design Repository	61
		4.2.3.	Contract Negotiation	61
		4.2.4.	API Implementation	62
		4.2.5.	Client Implementation	63
		4.2.6.	Discovery	63
		4.2.7.	Simulation	64
	4.3.	Language Features		64
	4.4.	Limitations		66
	4.5.	Summary		67

5. API Architectural Design Decisions   69

	5.1.	Requirements for APIs			69
		5.1.1.	Responsibilities of APIs		70
			5.1.1.1.	Gathering Data	70
			5.1.1.2.	Structuring and Formatting Data	70
			5.1.1.3.	Delivering Data	71
			5.1.1.4.	Securing and Protecting	71
		5.1.2.	Desirable Properties of APIs		71
			5.1.2.1.	Consumer-Centric	72
			5.1.2.2.	Simple	72
			5.1.2.3.	Clean	72
			5.1.2.4.	Clear	73
			5.1.2.5.	Approachable	73
			5.1.2.6.	Forgiving and Forward Compatible	73
			5.1.2.7.	Secure and Compliant	74
			5.1.2.8.	Performance, Scalable and Available	74
			5.1.2.9.	Reusable	74
			5.1.2.10.	Backward Compatible	74
		5.1.3.	Summary		75
	5.2.	Architectural Patterns			75
		5.2.1.	Client-Server Patterns		75
			5.2.1.1.	Stateful Server Pattern	76
			5.2.1.2.	Stateless Server Pattern	76

5

		5.2.2.	Facade Pattern	77
		5.2.3.	Proxy Pattern	78
	5.3.	Architectural Styles	79
		5.3.1.	REST Style	79
		5.3.2.	HATEOAS Style	80
		5.3.3.	RPC Style	81
			5.3.3.1. How does RPC work?	81
			5.3.3.2. JSON-RPC	81
			5.3.3.3. XML-RPC	81
		5.3.4.	SOAP Style	82
		5.3.5.	Streaming Style	82
	5.4.	Architectural Trade-offs	83
		5.4.1.	RPC in Comparison to REST	84
		5.4.2.	HATEOAS in Comparison to REST	85
		5.4.3.	SOAP in Comparison to REST	86
	5.5.	Summary	87

6. Introduction to REST　　　　　　　　　　　　　　　　89
	6.1.	HTTP	89
	6.2.	REST Concepts	91
		6.2.1.	Resource	91
		6.2.2.	API	92
		6.2.3.	Representation	92
		6.2.4.	Uniform Resource Interface	92
	6.3.	REST Constraints	93
	6.4.	State in REST	94
		6.4.1.	Application State	95
		6.4.2.	Resource State	95
		6.4.3.	Anti-Pattern: Using Token Attributes to Store Application State	96
		6.4.4.	Summary	96
	6.5.	Advantages of REST	97
	6.6.	HATEOAS Style	98
		6.6.1.	HATEOAS Concepts	98

		6.6.2.	HATEOAS Constraints	99
		6.6.3.	Advantages of HATEOAS	99
	6.7.	Summary		100

7. API Frontend Design Decisions   101

	7.1.	Resources		102
		7.1.1.	What is a Resource?	102
		7.1.2.	Instance Resources	104
		7.1.3.	Collection Resources	105
		7.1.4.	Controller Resources	106
		7.1.5.	Resource Ordering	107
			7.1.5.1. Root Resource	107
			7.1.5.2. Sub Resource	108
		7.1.6.	Resource Granularity	108
		7.1.7.	Resource Relations	109
			7.1.7.1. Option 1: Resource Ordering . .	110
			7.1.7.2. Option 2: IDs and Separate Root Resources	110
			7.1.7.3. Option 3: Links and Separate Root Resources	111
			7.1.7.4. Option 4: Embedded Resources	112
			7.1.7.5. Option 5: Combinations	113
		7.1.8.	Resource Links	113
		7.1.9.	Best Practices for Resource Design	114
			7.1.9.1. No Redundancy	114
			7.1.9.2. No Internal Data	115
			7.1.9.3. No Composite Resources	115
	7.2.	URI Design		115
		7.2.1.	Introduction	116
		7.2.2.	Recommendations	117
		7.2.3.	URI Template	118
		7.2.4.	Stable URIs	118
		7.2.5.	Nesting Depth	119
		7.2.6.	Maximum Length of URIs	119

	7.2.7.	URLs of Collections Resources	120
	7.2.8.	Relative URLs vs. Absolute URLs	120
7.3.	Representations		121
	7.3.1.	Where can Representations be Found? .	121
	7.3.2.	Content-Type of Representations	122
	7.3.3.	Addressing Representations	123
		7.3.3.1. Primitive Addressing of Representations	123
		7.3.3.2. Sophisticated Addressing of Representations	124
	7.3.4.	Content Negotiation	124
		7.3.4.1. Negotiating Content-Types . . .	126
		7.3.4.2. Negotiating Language	126
		7.3.4.3. Negotiating Character Encoding	127
		7.3.4.4. Negotiating Content Encoding .	127
	7.3.5.	Data Size of Representations	127
	7.3.6.	Binary Data	128
		7.3.6.1. Small Binary Data Elements . .	128
		7.3.6.2. Large Binary Data	128
	7.3.7.	JSON	129
		7.3.7.1. JSON Schema	130
		7.3.7.2. JSON to XML and back again .	130
		7.3.7.3. Common JSON Anti Patterns .	131
		7.3.7.4. JSONP	132
7.4.	Parameters		133
	7.4.1.	Use of Parameter Types	133
		7.4.1.1. Resource Creation and Update	134
		7.4.1.2. Resource Retrieval: Filtering and Sorting	134
		7.4.1.3. Resource Retrieval: Locators . .	135
		7.4.1.4. Resource Retrieval: Projections	136
		7.4.1.5. Resource Retrieval: Projection on Collection Resources	136

		7.4.1.6.	Resource Retrieval: Projection on	
			Instance Resources	137
		7.4.1.7.	Metadata	137
	7.4.2.	Parameter Types		137
		7.4.2.1.	Path Parameters	138
		7.4.2.2.	Query Parameters	138
		7.4.2.3.	Form Parameters.	139
		7.4.2.4.	Header Parameters	139

7.5. Methods 142
    7.5.1. Use of HTTP Methods 143
        7.5.1.1. Retrieve a Resource 143
        7.5.1.2. Create a new Resource 144
        7.5.1.3. Update a Resource 145
        7.5.1.4. Delete a Resource 146
        7.5.1.5. Check Existence of a Resource . 147
        7.5.1.6. Determine how to Call the API 147
        7.5.1.7. Test the Request 147
    7.5.2. Meaning of HTTP Methods 148
        7.5.2.1. GET 148
        7.5.2.2. POST 148
        7.5.2.3. PUT 149
        7.5.2.4. DELETE 149
        7.5.2.5. PATCH 150
        7.5.2.6. HEAD 151
        7.5.2.7. OPTIONS 151
        7.5.2.8. TRACE 151
        7.5.2.9. Non-Standard HTTP Methods . 152
    7.5.3. Properties of HTTP Methods 152
        7.5.3.1. Safe 153
        7.5.3.2. Idempotent 153

7.6. Status Codes 153
    7.6.1. Overview of HTTP Status Codes 154
    7.6.2. Redirection 155

9

	7.6.3.	Error Handling	156
		7.6.3.1. Client Errors	157
		7.6.3.2. Server Errors	158
		7.6.3.3. Error Message	159
7.7.	Input and Output Validation		160
	7.7.1.	Input Validation	160
	7.7.2.	Output Validation	162
7.8.	Intuitive Use		162
	7.8.1.	Consistent Names and Naming Schemes .	163
		7.8.1.1. Typical Naming Schemes	163
	7.8.2.	Summary	164
7.9.	Integration		164
	7.9.1.	Cross-Origin Resource Sharing (CORS) .	165
	7.9.2.	Browser Exploration	166
	7.9.3.	Robustness	167
	7.9.4.	Discovery	167

8. OpenAPI/Swagger for API Frontend Design — 169
    8.1. Introduction 169
    8.2. Root Element 172
    8.3. Resources 173
    8.4. Schema 175
    8.5. Parameters 177
    8.6. Reusable Elements 178
    8.7. Security 179
        8.7.1. Security Definition 179
        8.7.2. Security Binding 181

9. RAML for API Frontend Design — 183
    9.1. Introduction 183
    9.2. Root Element 185
    9.3. Schema 188
    9.4. Parameters 188
        9.4.1. Path Parameters 189

      9.4.2. Query Parameters 190
      9.4.3. Form Parameters 190
      9.4.4. Header Parameters 190
  9.5. Reusable Elements 191
      9.5.1. External Elements: Inclusion of Files . . . 191
      9.5.2. Internal Elements: Definition of Resource Types and Traits 191
      9.5.3. Internal Elements: Usage of Resource Types and Traits 192
  9.6. Security 192

10. API Backend Design Decisions   195
  10.1. Backends 196
  10.2. Transformations 197
      10.2.1. Transformation Source and Target 197
            10.2.1.1. Request Transformation 197
            10.2.1.2. Response Transformation 198
      10.2.2. Transformation Tasks 198
            10.2.2.1. Data Structure Transformation . 198
            10.2.2.2. Representation Transformation . 199
            10.2.2.3. Conversion between JSON and XML 199
            10.2.2.4. Security Mediation 201
      10.2.3. Transformation Tools 201
  10.3. Dealing with Backend Errors 202
  10.4. Logging 204
      10.4.1. Sanitizing Logged Data 204
      10.4.2. Require a Transaction ID / Request ID / Tracking ID 204

11. Non-Functional Properties of APIs   205
  11.1. Security 205
      11.1.1. The Appropriate Level of Security 205

- 11.1.2. Security Concerns 207
  - 11.1.2.1. Authentication 207
  - 11.1.2.2. Authorization 207
  - 11.1.2.3. Delegation 207
  - 11.1.2.4. Identity 208
  - 11.1.2.5. Attacks 208
  - 11.1.2.6. Integrity of API Input and Output 208
- 11.1.3. Security Mechanisms 208
  - 11.1.3.1. API Keys 208
  - 11.1.3.2. HTTP Basic 209
  - 11.1.3.3. HTTP Digest 210
  - 11.1.3.4. OAuth 212
  - 11.1.3.5. OpenID Connect and JWT . . . 213
  - 11.1.3.6. Access Restrictions by IP, Location and Time 214
  - 11.1.3.7. X.509 Transport Layer Security (TLS) 214
  - 11.1.3.8. Visibility Levels 215
  - 11.1.3.9. Validation 215
  - 11.1.3.10. Threat Protection 216
  - 11.1.3.11. Traffic Shaping 216
- 11.1.4. Security Best Practice 216
  - 11.1.4.1. Ensuring Confidentiality and Integrity of Information in URIs . 217
  - 11.1.4.2. Treat All APIs as Public APIs . 217
  - 11.1.4.3. Known Vulnerabilities and Known Attack Patterns 218
  - 11.1.4.4. Protect All APIs with OAuth by Default 218
  - 11.1.4.5. CORS 218
- 11.2. Performance and Availability 218
  - 11.2.1. Caching 219
  - 11.2.2. Traffic Shaping 219
  - 11.2.3. Pagination 220

11.2.4. Enable Content Compression 221
11.2.5. Remove Whitespace from Responses . . . 221
11.3. Caching 222
    11.3.1. Use Cases for Caching 222
        11.3.1.1. API-Side Caching 222
        11.3.1.2. Client-Side Caching 223
        11.3.1.3. What should be cached? 223
    11.3.2. Caching Mechanisms 224
    11.3.3. HTTP Caching Mechanism with Conditional Requests 224
        11.3.3.1. Determining if the Cached Data is Up to Date 225
        11.3.3.2. Reading Cached Data with Conditional GET 226
        11.3.3.3. Writing Cached Data with Conditional PUT and DELETE . . 227
        11.3.3.4. Cache-Control 228
11.4. Traffic Shaping 229
    11.4.1. Use Cases for Traffic Shaping 230
        11.4.1.1. Use Case: Protect API Platform 230
        11.4.1.2. Use Case: Protect Backends . . 230
        11.4.1.3. Use Case: Limit User Access . . 231
    11.4.2. Mechanisms for Traffic Shaping 231
        11.4.2.1. Rate Limitation 231
        11.4.2.2. Spike Limitation and Spike Smoothing 233
        11.4.2.3. Traffic Shaping with Quota . . . 234
11.5. Evolution and Versioning 235
    11.5.1. The Evolution Challenge 235
    11.5.2. Publication: The Root Cause of the Evolution Challenge 236
    11.5.3. Types of API Evolution 236
        11.5.3.1. Backward Compatible Changes . 236
        11.5.3.2. Incompatible Changes 237

　　　　　11.5.3.3. Conclusion of the Analysis . . . 238
　　　11.5.4. Anticipating and Avoiding Evolution . . . 238
　　　11.5.5. Coping with Evolution - Versioning 239
　　　　　11.5.5.1. Realize API Versioning in Accept
　　　　　　　　　 Header 239
　　　　　11.5.5.2. Realize API Versioning as URI
　　　　　　　　　 Path Parameter 240
　　　　　11.5.5.3. Realize API Versioning in a Custom HTTP Header 240
　　　　　11.5.5.4. Realize API Versioning as Query
　　　　　　　　　 Parameter 241
　　　　　11.5.5.5. Realize API Versioning as a new
　　　　　　　　　 Subdomain 241
　　　　　11.5.5.6. HATEOAS Versioning via Links 241
　　　11.5.6. Supporting Multiple Versions Simultaneously 242

12. API Client Design　　　　　　　　　　　　　　　243
　　12.1. Designing the Solution 243
　　　12.1.1. Functionality in the Client or in the API? 244
　　　12.1.2. Use an existing API or build a new API? 245
　　　12.1.3. How to choose a third party API? 245
　　　　　12.1.3.1. Step 1: Find and Discovering the
　　　　　　　　　 API 245
　　　　　12.1.3.2. Step 2: Test the API 246
　　　　　12.1.3.3. Step 3: Use the API and Learn
　　　　　　　　　 about the API 247
　　　　　12.1.3.4. Step 4: Learn about the API Provider 247
　　12.2. Discovering APIs 248
　　　12.2.1. Consumer Discovery 248
　　　12.2.2. Automatic Discovery 249
　　12.3. Calling APIs 250
　　　12.3.1. Prepare and Send the API Request 250
　　　12.3.2. Process the API Response 251

A. Appendix — 255
- A.1. Feedback 255
- A.2. About the Author 255
- A.3. Other Products by the Author 256
  - A.3.1. Online Course on RESTful API Design . 256
  - A.3.2. Book on API Architecture 257
  - A.3.3. Online Course on API Security with OAuth 2.0 258
  - A.3.4. Book on API Security with OAuth 2.0 .. 258

B. Typical Content-Types — 261

C. HTTP Methods — 263

D. HTTP Headers — 265

E. HTTP Status Codes — 271

1. Introduction

1.1. What is an API?

Software is typically used by people like you and me via a user interface. Increasingly, however, software is not only used by people, but also by other software applications. This requires another type of interface, an Application Programming Interface, in short API.

APIs offer a simple way for connecting to, integrating with and extending a software system. More precisely, APIs are used for building distributed software systems, whose components are loosely coupled. The APIs studied here are web-APIs, which deliver data resources via a web technology stack. Typical applications using APIs are mobile apps, cloud apps, web applications or smart devices.

The charm of APIs is that they are simple, clean, clear and approachable. They provide a reusable interface that different applications can connect to easily. However, APIs do not offer a user interface, they are usually not visible on the surface and typically no end user will directly interact with them. Instead, APIs operate under the hood and are only directly called by other applications. APIs are used for machine to machine communication and for the integration of two or more software systems.

The only people interacting with APIs directly are the developers creating applications or solutions with the APIs. This is why APIs need to be built with the developers in mind, who will integrate the APIs into new applications. This insight explains, why a new perspective is required for building APIs.

1.2. Why APIs?

An API offers a simple way for connecting to, integrating with and extending software systems. Now, think about the entities that are run by software. Businesses, markets and banks are run by software. Industrial production processes are controlled by software. Machines, cars and many consumer products contain software. However, these software systems are typically isolated and functionality of one system cannot be accessed from the other system. APIs provide a possibility to connect these separate software entities. APIs provide the capabilities which are essential for connecting, extending and integrating software. And by connecting software, APIs connect businesses with other businesses, businesses with their products, services with products or products directly with other products.

The infrastructure for enabling this connection is already in place. Each and every person, each employee and each customer has a smart, internet-enabled device, businesses have websites and web-services. Even an increasing number of the products sold by the businesses carry digital sensors and are internet enabled. All these devices are connected to the internet and can – in principle – be connected via APIs.

Just one example for the business to business integration: The business of an enterprise can be expanded by linking the business to partners up and down the value chain. Since businesses are run by IT, the businesses can be better linked by integrating the IT systems of a business up and down the value chain to the IT systems of other businesses, partners, employees and to customers. This can be accomplished if the IT systems of the business partners are linked via services.

An enterprise cannot force its business partners to use its services. But it can make these services so good – so valuable and simple – that the business partners will want to use them. If these services are good, they can become a means for retaining existing partners and a means for obtaining new partners. But what makes a service good? In this context a service is good ...

- ... if it is valuable and helps the partners perform their business.
- ... if it fits the exact needs of the partners.
- ... if it is simple to understand.
- ... if it is easy to integrate and monitor for the partners.
- ... if it is secure, reliable and meets the performance requirements.

APIs should fulfill all of the above conditions. This is why they are used for both external integration with business partners and for internal integration within the company. Amazon, for example, uses APIs internally, to integrate the IT systems of its departments. If the interfaces and technology are already in place for internal integration, it becomes easier to provide external integration. External integration is used with business partners or external entities. External APIs are also necessary for realizing mobile apps. Interesting mobile apps use company data, data that is delivered to the app via APIs.

Another reason for using APIs is their use as an innovation lab of the enterprise. To fulfill this vision, the API portfolio should enable the enterprise to build innovative apps with little effort and spark creativity. By making company assets easily available through API, new uses of these assets can be found. Since APIs provide a new, simple way for accessing company assets, assets can be used in new ways within the company. Providing external access to the assets of your organization via APIs, enables external third party developers to create innovations for your organization by using your organization's assets.

1.3. How are APIs used?

APIs are one component in a typical internet solution. A typical internet solution consists of an app, APIs and backend systems. The app is offered to end users. However, the end-user does not call the API directly. Instead, the API is called by the app.

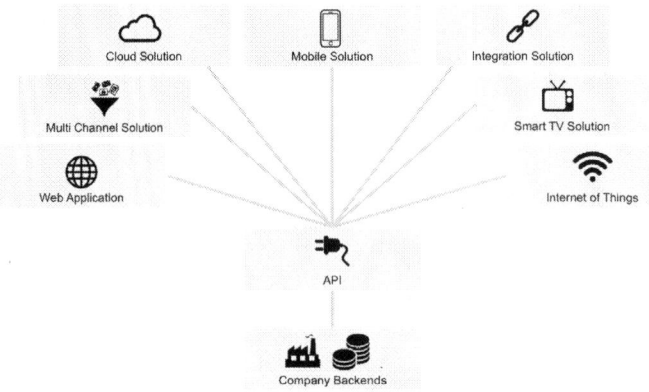

Figure 1.1.: API-based Solutions

As shown in Figure 1.1, an API-based solution typically consists of:

- A client or app (mobile app, web app, cloud app, TV app or IoT device) that calls the APIs and processes the data provided by the APIs. This client is responsible for the end user experience.

- A number of APIs that provide data to the app.

- An API platform that manages the APIs and connects the API to the backend systems.

- Backend systems, which implement the business logic, store the data or run the algorithms.

1.4. What is API Design?

Any type of design requires taking well-informed decisions. The decisions are intended to make the product better in some way, e.g. provide more functionality, provide better quality or a better user experience. Better design decisions typically lead to better products. This is no different when designing APIs. Which design decisions are there for APIs? We see four groups of design decisions.

- **Architectural Design Decisions:** When designing an API, decisions have to be made regarding architectural issues, such as the patterns and the styles to be used. Should the API follow the REST or SOAP architectural style? These design decisions are foundational and have an impact on all following decisions. We will address architectural design decisions for APIs in chapter 5.

- **API Frontend Design Decisions:** Since the frontend of the API is visible to the API consumers (= customers of the API), frontend design decisions are quite critical for the success of an API. Frontend design for APIs is typically RESTful design. For RESTful frontend design we need to answer questions such as: How does the URI of the API look like? Are the parameters passed in the form of query parameters or path parameters? Which headers and status codes should be used? We will address frontend design decisions for APIs in chapter 7.

- **API Backend Design Decisions:** The functionality of the API depends on leveraging data and services of backend systems. Backend design decisions address the connection between API and backend. Design decisions regarding the integration, transformation, aggregation, security and error handling of the backend have an impact on the functionality of the API. We will address backend design decisions for APIs in chapter 10.

- **Non-functional Design Decisions:** The architectural, frontend and backend design decisions are primarily taken to craft the functionality of the API. However, these decisions also have an impact on the non-functional properties of the API, such as security, performance, availability, and evolvability. Non-functional properties of the API should not be an afterthought. The API needs to be designed right from the start to fulfill non-functional requirements. We will address non-functional design decisions for APIs in chapter 11.

In this book we address all four groups of design decisions for APIs. The focus is, however, on REST and the API frontend design decisions.

1.5. What is the difference between API Design and API Architecture?

In general, API architecture spans the bigger picture of APIs and can be seen from several perspectives:

API architecture may refer to the architecture of the complete solution, consisting not only of the API itself, but also of an API client such as a mobile app and several other components. API solution architecture explains the components and their relations within the software solution.

API architecture may refer to the technical architecture of the API platform. When building, running and exposing not only one, but several APIs, it becomes clear that certain building blocks of the API, runtime functionality and management functionality for the API need to be used over and over again. An API platform provides an infrastructure for developing, running and managing APIs.

API architecture may refer to the architecture of the API portfolio. The API portfolio contains all APIs of the enterprise and needs to be managed like a product. API portfolio architecture analyzes the functionality of the API and organizes, manages and reuses the APIs.

API architecture may refer to the design decisions for a particular API. This is what we usually refer to as API proxy architecture. It includes architectural design decisions, non-functional design decisions, frontend and backend design decisions. To document these design decisions, API description languages are used.

So, what is the difference between API architecture and API design? API design is one aspect of API architecture. API architecture has a wider scope, considering also the API solution, API platform and API portfolio. In a way, the API architecture defines the frame, in which API design can take place and does make sense.

API design can only be effective if the overall API architecture is already in place. In this book we assume that this is the case and focus only on the aspect of API design. If you are interested in the big picture of API architecture, I recommend the book "API Architecture" from the API-University Series [2].

1.6. Why is API Design important?

For a moment, picture the Golden Gate Bridge. I think you would agree, that it is very hard to move the pillars of such a bridge, which is made of steel and concrete. Such changes would be difficult, costly and time intensive. This is why engineers design a blueprint before building the bridge. The design allows for planning all the details, iterating over several proposals and performing what-if analysis. Changes to the design are easy and cheap to perform. And by making changes to the design, it hopefully becomes unnecessary to make changes to the real artifacts. The same is true for APIs.

When APIs have already been built, changes are difficult, expensive and time-intensive. Even worse, the changes to published APIs might break any clients using the API. The consumers might get upset and switch the API provider. To avoid this scenario, the API needs to be right from the start, by the first time it is published, and API design can contribute to this goal.

An appropriate API frontend design enables a contract-first design approach. Once the frontend design is externalized and written down (e.g. in RAML or OpenAPI/Swagger), it can be used not only by the API providers to implement the API proxy, but also by API consumers to build apps with this API. The API consumer does not have to wait for the API to be finished, but development of API and app can proceed in parallel.

Non-functional properties of the API should not be an afterthought. The API needs to be designed right from the start to fulfill all non-functional properties such as security, performance and availability.

API design forces us to think about the API before we build it. It helps us to avoid building the wrong API, or building the API in the wrong way. Building APIs in the wrong way is not ideal, but it is not critical. Building the wrong API is way more critical. In the worst case, there are no consumers for the newly built APIs. How can this happen? It happens, because the needs of the API consumers are not known and the requirements are unclear. If the requirements are unclear and there are just some vague assumptions, one has to meet with potential API consumers and ask them for their needs. In this situation, it can be helpful if the API provider is also be the API consumer. In this situation, the API providers have to "eat their own dog food". The change of perspective that goes along the strategy helps the API provider to understand what it feels like to use the own API. Inconveniences, missing features, missing data or missing documentation can be discovered quite effectively in this way. Learn more about the contract-first design approach in chapter 3.

1.7. Why should I build RESTful APIs?

Great products are designed with rigorous customer focus, a deep understanding of the customers, their needs and desires. And with these ingredients, great customer experiences can be designed around a product.

To design great APIs, you first need to realize, that APIs are in fact products. APIs are products of their own! So who are the customers of your API? APIs are never exposed to end-users directly, but they still have customers. The customers are the developers of the API consumer. So when creating a great customer experience, you in fact need to create a great developer experience (more on this in chapter 2).

This is where REST comes into the picture. REST makes it easy to create a great developer experience. REST imposes a couple of architectural constraints on your API design.

Constraints are often seen as a limitation; but in fact they are not - they are a help for the designer. Regard the REST constraints not as a limitation, but rather as a support for building great APIs, i.e. APIs that are simple, clear, clean and approachable.

Of course, you need to know about these REST constraints and how to use them. We explain these constraints and show their practical application in chapters 6 and 7.

1.8. Why do I need OpenAPI, Swagger or RAML?

Once an API has been designed, it needs to be communicated to team members, developers, product managers, architects, testers and of course to the consumers. API design is often used to communicate between designer and developer or to communicate between provider and consumer. In a sense, the API design serves as a contract.

So the question is: How can I write down my API design? The answer is: API description languages, such as the OpenAPI/Swagger or RAML. They can be used for expressing important aspects of the API design. Especially the frontend design decisions and architectural design decisions, which are visible to the consumer, can be captured by API description languages.

API description languages are also very powerful tools, that can be used for improving the efficiency of design and development (see chapter 3) through automated generation of design and development artifacts. For example, they can be used for code generation of the API, code generation of the API clients, generation of documentation, generation of tests, and the generation of mocks.

Learn more about API description languages in chapter 4, about OpenAPI/Swagger in chapter 8 and about RAML in chapter 9.

1.9. How to put API Design into Practice?

Design is nice, but you need to deliver running software? Yes, running software is where the rubber meets the road. To become useful, the API design needs to be put into practice: the design needs to be implemented. An API design approach provides practical guidelines and explains how to develop an API design into an API implementation that consumers can use. In this book I will show you how proper API design can get you to reliable, stable and beautiful APIs.

I promise, I will get back to APIs in a moment. For now, let us assume that we were in the car manufacturing business and we would like to build a new car. What would we have to do?

1. We find out, how the consumer would want to use the new car. We design the car, so it fits into the portfolio of different models that our company sells - sports cars, vans and trucks.

2. We choose the architectural style, i.e. if the car uses a diesel engine, hybrid engine or a fully electric engine.

3. We design a blueprint of the car according to the consumer's needs and wants.

4. We simulate components of the car and build a prototype. We test the prototype, collect feedback, adapt and iterate. Iteratively the car is improved.

5. Finally, we configure the assembly line for putting all the car parts together efficiently.

And what would the corresponding steps be, when building an API?

1. We find out, how the majority of consumers would want to use the new API. We design the API, so it fits into the

portfolio of different APIs that our company offers. See chapter 2.

2. We choose the architectural style, i.e. if the API applies a REST, RPC or SOAP style. See chapter 5.

3. We design a blueprint of the API using an API description language (see chapter 4), such as RAML (see chapter 9) or Swagger (see chapter 8).

4. We design the visible frontend interface (see chapter 7) and design the backend interface (see chapter 10). We build a prototype of the API and simulate its behavior. We collect feedback on the design, check that the design fulfills the non-functional properties (see chapter 11). Based on the feedback we adapt and iterate. Iteratively the API design is improved.

5. Finally, we use a generative API design approach (see chapter 3) to develop APIs efficiently. Think of the API design approach as an assembly line! Automate as much as possible. API description languages (see chapter 4) will help you with this task. Of course, the generative techniques are only used as far as possible, at some point some code might still need to be written.

The API design approach we propose is a consumer-oriented approach, which also incorporates ideas of contract-first design, agile approaches and simulation. In this design approach, the contract is expressed in the form of an API description. In each step of the design approach, an API description is either created, refined or used: the API description is the red thread connecting all the steps of the design approach.

2. Consumer-Oriented API Design: APIs as Products

APIs are often built according to the ideas of the API provider without considering the needs and wishes of potential API consumers. Investing time and energy in building an API that no one wants is a waste of resources. It is a big mistake that can be avoided easily. Maybe it is a no-brainer for you, but I have seen this mistake so many times, that I need to make the importance absolutely clear and propose an approach for avoiding the mistake.

I propose to engage with potential API consumers before and during the design of the API and call the approach *Consumer-Oriented API Design*. So what does Consumer-Oriented API Design mean and why is it so important? What are the implications of it? And how do we do it? You will find out in this chapter.

2.1. APIs are Products

To design great APIs, we first need to realize, that APIs are in fact products. APIs are products that are offered on a market to satisfy the needs of a group of customers.

This means that APIs are not individually created integration solutions that are tailored for a particular customer and a particular use case. Instead, APIs are designed as generic products for a group of customers. They are intended to be highly *reusable* software. In this way APIs can provide solutions to common needs and challenges that are shared by many customers. It may be, that the idea for an API originates from one particular use case for one particular customer, but successful APIs are always more generic. There is always a group of customers, who is interested in solving their diverse use cases with the API.

I like to compare APIs to Lego bricks. The manufacturer usually sells the bricks with an instruction manual, which describes one particular use case, one way of building something with these bricks, let's say a fire truck. But the bricks are pretty generic: the same bricks can be composed in new ways, that have never been imagined by the manufacturer. So the bricks that were used to build the fire truck, can be used to build a spaceship, castle or racing car.

Why is this possible? It is possible, because the bricks are reusable products, just like APIs. And the bricks are reusable, because they have a simple, clean, clear and approachable interface, just like well-designed APIs.

2.2. API Consumers

Great products typically have a great customer experience. They are designed with rigorous customer focus, a deep understanding of the customers and compassion for both the needs and desires of the customers.

So who are the customers of your API? What do these customers have in common? What is a great customer experience for them? And why do they want to use your API?

The customers of your API are the consumers of the API - the developers building API-based solutions. API consumers are developers, using APIs to build other products (e.g. mobile apps, cloud apps) for end users. APIs are never exposed to end-users directly, only to API consumers.

Since the customers of your API are developers, the customer experience should be targeted towards them. So when creating a great customer experience, you in fact need to create a great *developer experience*! A great developer experience requires an API, that is both functional and well-designed - an API that is easy to use, easy to integrate, well-documented and easy to get started with. In this book we will discuss how to create such well-designed APIs.

The group of API consumers is likely a different one for each and every API you build. So you actually need to figure out the characteristics of your API customer group for each API you build.

You want to look at API consumers as a group, never a single API consumer. Why? Because you want to build APIs as products, with a high potential for reuse by many different consumers.

2.3. Consumer-Oriented APIs

API consumers can often choose from a selection of alternative APIs with similar functionality. These APIs are offered by different API providers, meaning that only one API provider "can make the deal" with a particular API consumer. So if the functionality of the offered APIs is similar, how do consumers choose APIs?

Consumers often end up choosing the API that is easy to use, easy to integrate, well-documented and easy to get started with. This means: *Your API should be as simple, clean, clear and approachable as possible from the perspective of the API consumer.*

But, isn't this subjective, you might say? What looks simple, clean, clear and approachable from one angle, might not be simple from another perspective. This is why it is important to design and evaluate APIs from the perspective of the API consumers. It is their perspective as customers of the API that matters. So if you as an API provider don't know the opinion and perspective of your API consumers, you need to figure it out and you need to ask them what it means for them when an API is simple, clean, clear and approachable.

At the same time, keep in mind that APIs are products and should be *reusable*. They should not be built for a particular API consumer, but for a group of API consumers with similar needs. So ideally, you would ask multiple API consumers.

2.4. Building Consumer-Oriented APIs

You probably instantly know, when you have a great API in front of you. But how do you build one? What are the tasks for building consumer oriented APIs?

You need to identify the target consumers (see section 2.4.1), engage with them (see section 2.4.2), get to know their needs and learn about the problems they are trying to solve with the API. This can be achieved by understanding the architecture of the consumers' solution (see section 2.4.3).

These tasks are described in this section. They allow you to understand the perspective of an API consumer. And from this perspective you can then start to design your API (see chapter 3).

2.4.1. Identify the Prototypical API Consumers

You first need to identify the key consumers of your API. Sometimes you don't know from the beginning who the consumers are, or what they want. Sometimes you might only gradually find out, who the API consumers are and what their needs are. Ideally you have a pilot group of API consumers that can act as a sounding board for your API design.

But keep in mind, that you develop the API as a product – not as a custom integration solution for a certain consumer. Your goal is to develop a reusable API, that can be used by many consumers in many different scenarios and applications.

To avoid falling into the trap of building a custom solution, it is your task to distinguish between the needs and requirements of a particular consumer and the needs and requirements that the majority of consumers will have. Often it is helpful to construct a *prototypical API consumer* from the common needs of the API consumers.

2.4.2. Engage with API Consumers

When people ask me how to design a successful API, I usually ask back: "What do you need to do, so your consumers think that your API is simple, clean, clear and approachable?" Ask your consumers about their preferences. Know your consumers and know their idea of a clean, clear and approachable API. Just ask them. The answers will guide you towards a consumer-oriented API, which is much more likely to become successful. You can run the engagement with API consumers like a classical requirements engineering process. Alternatively, you may use more interactive techniques such as design thinking, to uncover hidden needs, to allow for more creativity and to find unexpected solutions.

2.4.3. Learn about the Solution Architecture of Consumers

It is essential to learn about the solution architecture of your consumers. Become clear on which problems they tackle, which solutions they want to build and what they expect from your API.

The starting point for a consumer-centric API is an analysis of what is needed by the consumers. This might seem quite natural when reading it, but all too often when it is time for designing and implementing, it is forgotten. We need to force ourselves to find out about the needs of the API consumers. This allows us to design an optimal experience for the interaction between the consumer and the API. For the API provider it is thus important to ask: What would the consumer want to achieve by using the API? How can I make it easy for the consumer to find the API? How can I help the consumer to build apps with my API and make it convenient for the consumer to use the API?

What does that mean in practice? The consumers are outside the organization of the API provider, thus the API provider needs to start the design process outside her organization. Only in the last step of this approach, the API provider may make considerations about what is inside the organization: the data formats, and the connections to existing backends. This approach certainly means more work on the side of the API provider, but there is a larger chance that the consumer gets a better API.

2.5. Summary

Design your API as a product that is reusable by various consumers and in various use cases. You need to know your prototypical API consumers, their needs and their solution architectures. Your API should be as simple, clean, clear and approachable as possible from their perspective, the perspective of the prototypical API consumers. If you design APIs as reusable products and design them from the perspective of the prototypical API consumers, then you build consumer-oriented APIs – APIs that your consumers will love.

3. API Design and Development Approach

This chapter is supposed to provide an answer to the question: How should I design and develop my APIs? Many approaches for proper API design and development have been proposed and are still the subject of passionate debates. There is no right or wrong approach, but there is an approach that fits into a specific company culture better than others. This is why we present a API design and development approach consisting of some coarse granular phases that you can pick and choose from to ensure that the approach you use for your company actually fits your company culture. This is one of the best ways to make sure that the API approach is actually accepted and applied by the team. Look at the proposed approach as a guideline, which provides some goalposts along the way, that were constructed based on past failures, experiences and learnings.

3.1. Foundations

In the proposed API approach we use best practices for design, such as consumer-oriented design, contract-first design, iterative design and simulation-based design. In the following we introduce these best practices and show why and how they apply to API design.

3.1.1. Consumer-Oriented Design Approach

There are two basic methodological approaches. They are known under the names inside-out approach and outside-in approach, depending on the starting point and the direction of the design process. We propose the outside-in approach because it is consumer-oriented. We mention the inside-out approach as well to contrast and clarify the differences.

3.1.1.1. Inside-out Approach

The starting point for the inside-out approach is an analysis of what already exists inside the organization of the API provider. For API providers, the backend systems already exist inside the organization and are used as a basis for defining the API. The design of an API developed with the inside-out approach will closely resemble the structure of the backend system. Using this approach, an API could be built just by forwarding calls to backends, optionally some data format transformations and some protocol transformations.

This approach is quite simple from the perspective of the API provider, since the functional scope of the API is confined by one backend system. The complexities of aggregating information from multiple backend systems are reduced. For the API provider this approach might seem to be the natural choice.

Even though building the API may be simple from the perspective of the API provider, it might be quite complex to use the API for the API consumers, since they are confronted with the complex data structures of the backends. Such an API is not likely to be consumer-oriented.

3.1.1.2. Outside-in Approach

In a way, the outside-in approach is the opposite to the inside-out approach. The starting point for the outside-in approach is an analysis of what is needed by the consumers. The consumers are outside the organization of the API provider, thus the API provider needs to start the design process outside her organization. Only in the last step of this approach, the API provider may make considerations about what is inside the organization: the data formats, and the connections to existing backends.

The consumer-oriented approach described in chapter 2 is an outside-in approach. So why is a consumer-oriented API important? A measure for the success of an API initiative is the wide-spread use of the API: the API should be used by as many consumers as possible. To maximize the uptake of APIs with potential consumers, to maximize the active usage of the API and to maximize the integration in third party apps, the API needs to be as simple as possible from the perspective of the consumer. It certainly means more work on the side of the API provider, but there is a bigger chance that the consumer gets an API, she actually like to use.

The basic idea of the outside-in approach is to focus on the consumers. One needs to identify the target consumers first and then get to know their needs. This allows for designing an optimal experience for the interaction between the consumer and the API. For the API provider it is thus important to ask: What would the consumer want to achieve by using the API? How can I make it easy for the consumer to find the API? How can I help the consumer to build apps with my API and make it convenient for the consumer to use the API? Check out chapter 2 for the details of this approach.

3.1.2. Contract-First Design Approach

In contract-first design, the central artifact is an explicit contract between API provider and API consumer. Such a contract is either dictated by the provider – or better – it is specified by provider and consumer together. In this contract, the API provider guarantees to provide APIs to the consumer, exactly as they were specified in the contract. Based on this contract, the consumer can already start implementing a solution before having access to the API.

3.1.3. Agile Design Approach

Agility is based on the premise that you can start without having a full set of specs. You can always adapt and change the specs later, as you go and as you have learned more. Through multiple iterations, architectural design can converge to the right solution. If the iterations are performed based on the architectural blueprint and not based on a full implementation, architecture improves the overall efficiency of development. But, is the agile approach 100% compatible with the requirements for APIs?

Before publishing the API, the API can be changed without constraints and the agile approach can be used. Change is easy and possible at any time.

After publishing the API, it becomes more difficult to realize changes. If a published API changes, clients may break. New versions need to be created for each API change that is not backward compatible. The interface specs are fully defined and thus the prerequisites for agility are no longer given. See section 11.5 for more details on evolution and versioning of APIs.

An agile approach should only be used, until the API is published for the first time. Once the API has been published, changes need to be controlled more strictly and agility is confined to new versions of the API.

3.1.4. Simulation-based Design

Basically every software system has dependencies to other software, such as other software components, libraries and frameworks. Due to these dependencies, some components cannot be developed until the development of their dependencies has been completed. The consequence is sequential development of the components, a long development time and a long time-to market for the complete software system.

Simulations offer a solution: they make it possible to break up the dependencies between software components and allow for integration and development of software components, even though their dependencies have not been developed, yet. Dependencies are replaced by simulations.

In API design there are two use cases for simulations:

- The simulation of backend systems allows for developing APIs without fully implemented backend systems.

- The simulation of APIs allows for developing apps (or other API solutions) without fully implemented APIs.

Both types of simulations have their place in API design - but in different scenarios. In the following sections we look at each of these two types of simulations in more detail.

3.1.4.1. Simulation of Backends

Since APIs depend on the backend systems and their behavior, the implementation of an API can only start after the backend has become available. If the backend has not been finalized yet, the development of the API is blocked and the API cannot be built.

Simulations of backend systems can be used to support the development of APIs. Backend simulations break the dependencies from APIs to backends. If the real backend is not available yet, a simulation of the backend can be used in its place. Since the behavior of the simulation is the same as the behavior of the real backend, the implementation of the API with a simulated backend can proceed independently of the availability of the implementation of the backend.

3.1.4.2. Simulation of the API

The development of an API solution, such as a mobile app, depends on the availability of the included APIs. If the APIs are not available, the development of the mobile app is blocked.

Simulations of APIs can support the development of mobile apps, which depend on the APIs. Even though the API has not been implemented yet, the mobile app can be built and the API can be integrated. The development of the API and the development of the mobile app can take place in parallel. The simulation speeds up the development time of the overall API solution, and allows for short time to market.

Simulation-based design of APIs and the contract-first design for APIs actually go hand-in-hand. The contract for the API can be used as a specification for the simulation.

3.1.5. Conclusion

An API solution has a certain complexity. Complexity does not simply go away – it has to be handled somewhere, by someone. Thus, the complexity of the API solution can either be dealt with in the client or in the API.

If the complexity is dealt with in the client, the task of the API provider is simple and the task of the API consumer is difficult. This is usually the result of the inside-out approach and leads to sub-optimal APIs that make the life of the API consumer unnecessarily hard.

If the complexity is dealt with in the API, the task of the API provider is difficult. However, the task of the API consumer is simple. This is usually the result of the outside-in approach. An outside-in approach has a higher chance of producing APIs that consumers love and despite the difficulties for the API provider, it is the recommended approach.

Since building consumer-oriented APIs with the outside-in approach is rather difficult for the API provider, as much methodological support as possible should be given to the API provider. This includes contract-first design, agile design and simulation-based design.

Applying the contract-first ideas to API design, allows for a clear separation of the responsibility between API and client.

Applying an agile approach can help to navigate in situations with unclear or vague requirements, but should only be applied until the API is published.

Applying ideas of the simulation approach allows for breaking up the dependencies during development. It allows for an independent development of client and API, despite the dependencies between them.

Our proposed API design approach, which is described in the following section, integrates ideas from all of these approaches.

3.2. Design Approach

This design approach is an outside-in approach and also incorporates ideas of contract-first design, the agile approach and simulation-based development. In this approach, the contract is expressed in the form of an API description. In each step of the approach, an API description is either created, refined or used: the API description is the red thread connecting all the steps of the approach.

3.2.1. Overview

Let's start with an overview of the phases in this API design approach. Each phase of this approach consists of a creative part and a verification part. During the creative part an artifact is crafted, during the verification part early feedback on the artifact is collected. In each phase along the design and development journey, feedback from the consumers is elicited. It is important to collect the feedback as early as possible, when changes to the API are still possible, relatively simple and can be implemented with low risk, low effort and low costs.

This design approach is meant to be used iteratively. There are small iterations, which are triggered by the verification part of the same phase. And there are also big iterations, which are triggered by one of the later verification phases and require going back to the creative part of an earlier phase. Keep in mind, that in an iterative and agile approach, not all information and requirements about the constructed artifact need to be available in the beginning, but new and more detailed information and insights are gathered and integrated during each iteration.

Our proposed API design approach is organized in the following six phases:

- Phase 1: Domain Analysis
- Phase 2: Architectural Design
- Phase 3: Prototyping
- Phase 4: Implementing for Production
- Phase 5: Publishing
- Phase 6: Maintenance

In sections 3.2.2 to 3.2.7 we look at each phase of the API design approach in more detail.

3.2.2. Phase 1: Domain Analysis

The goal of the first phase is to analyze the "problem domain", identify resources and sketch a simple API description for each resource. This API description can be verified by simulation and integration into a demo app.

The first step of a domain analysis phase is gaining some clarity on the needs of the consumer and possible usage scenarios. Sketching usage scenarios is a creative act. It is a good idea to involve multiple and diverse stakeholders in this initial brainstorming phase.

Start by asking yourself:

- Who are the consumers of the API?

- What is the purpose of the API?

- Which API solutions do the consumers plan to build with the API?

- Which other API solutions would be possible with the API?

Even though the development of new APIs is usually triggered by a concrete project, the goal should be the development of a generic API. Thus, not only the usage scenario at hand, or the obvious usage scenario should be sketched. Ideally, a broad set of usage scenarios for the API should be sketched. Sketching can be either in some form of graphics or in the form of text.

The next step is to build a resource taxonomy for the given usage scenarios. Think from a consumer's perspective about the usage scenario, try not to have the tinted view of some existing backend structure or existing database tables, since those provide an internal view. Take on the view of the API consumer. How would an API look like that she wants to use? What apps would the consumer want to build? What data objects would the consumer want to use in her apps?

To create a taxonomy, write down the usage scenario, then select the nouns in the text. Shortlist the nouns that would make sense as resources, i.e. nouns that describe data objects, which the operations create, read, update or delete can be performed on. As part of the taxonomy creation, one needs to analyze the relationships between the resources:

A dependent resource cannot exist without the other. An independent resource on the other hand can exist without any other resource. Associative resources exist independently but still have some kind of relation, e.g. they may be connected by reference. The next step is to think about the states of the resources and possible transitions between the resource states.

The resources in the taxonomy have states and during the execution of the app, the resources may change their states and transition into new states. Express the states and transitions in a state diagram.

Which insights can we gather from the state diagram? The states provide an indicator for the resources that are needed. The transitions in the diagram provide an indicator for the HTTP methods that need to be supported.

With the information collected during domain analysis, a first API description can be built with an API description language (see chapter 4). Admittedly, this first iteration of an API description is rather a sketch than an architecture, but it still allows defining the taxonomy, the API resources and their operations.

3.2.2.1. Verification of Phase 1: Simulation & Demo App

A good simulation allows us to answer some questions about a planned system without having to spend all the effort of building that system. At this stage, the simulation can help to define the purpose of the API: Does it make sense to build an API with the given functionality for the usage scenarios at hand? Does the sketched API help me build the solution? Are the requirements of the API properly captured in the API description?

To answer these questions, a first, low-fidelity API prototype should be built. Such an early prototype should only be built, when the effort for creating the prototype is minimal. This is why the API prototype should not be implemented manually, but it should be constructed automatically by generating a simulation based on the API description. Frameworks for API description languages offer such capabilities for generating simulations.

The simulation provides a verification of the stand-alone API. Even more effective would be a verification of the API in the context of an app or solution. This is not necessarily an app with real requirements. A simple demo app for an artificial problem is sufficient for this phase. The simplest demo app would be a little bit more than a curl call. The demo app provides a showcase for the API and can be reused in later stages.

3.2.3. Phase 2: Architectural and Frontend Design

During the architectural design phase, the API description created in phase 1, is refined. First of all, an appropriate architectural style should be chosen, such as REST, RPC or HATEOAS (see chapter 5).

These design decisions should be documented by refining and updating the API description. The API description thus becomes an evolving, single source of truth about the current state of the system.

Once the bigger-picture, architectural design decisions are nailed, frontend design decisions can be handled (see chapter 7). For the REST architectural style, these design decisions include:

- Resources

- URIs

- Representations

- Parameters

- HTTP methods
- HTTP status codes
- Consistent naming
- Validation

The detailed design decisions are documented by refining the API description. Typically OpenAPI/Swagger (see chapter 8) or RAML (see chapter 9) are used as API description languages. In addition to the above design decisions, it should be avoided to reinvent the wheel for common APIs. Instead, published or company-specific API templates should be used. APIs should also be designed as a part of the API portfolio, meaning that the designed API should be consistent with the other APIs in the same portfolio.

3.2.3.1. Verification of Phase 2: Simulation & Demo App

A simulation should be used at this point to quickly verify the effects of the architectural and detailed design decisions. The following questions might help to verify the design: Is the API still easy to use? Is it still a small, agile and usable API or did we create a monster API? Does this API help us to realize our usage scenarios? Does the API follow the architectural style selected?

Ideally, the changes that are necessary to the API description at this stage are minimal. The API description should become stable.

As part of the verification, the API description can be handed over to pilot consumers, so they can base the design of their API solution, such as their mobile app, on our design. The demo app created in the previous phase can be reused for integration testing of the simulated API.

3.2.4. Phase 3: Prototyping

> Plan to throw one away;
> you will anyhow.
>
> *Frederick P. Brooks*

Prototyping is a preparation phase for the productive implementation. One goal of prototyping is to learn as many practical insights as possible while spending as little effort as possible. This can be achieved by quickly creating a simple prototype implementation, that you plan to throw away. Not every aspect of the API should be implemented in this phase, but only the critical aspects of the API are assessed. Assessment of the prototype is performed from a technical perspective by the engineers and from a usability perspective by pilot consumers. Typical design decisions that are explored during prototyping are the backend design decisions (see chapter 10) and non-functional properties of the system (see chapter 11).

There are thus two goals for proper prototyping: practical insights into critical implementation and usability issues and a low effort for the creation of the prototype.

The first goal is to gain practical insights through the prototyping effort. To gain some learning with practical relevance, the API prototype needs to be as realistic as possible. While simulations can be considered to be low-fidelity prototypes, this phase creates high-fidelity prototypes that are more realistic, more relevant and closer to the actual implementation. The API prototype should conform to the API description and use real data from real backends.

At the same time, there is the second goal, which requires the prototype to be built as quickly as possible and with as little effort and budget as possible. To achieve the necessary speed, the implementation does not have to be pretty, does not have to be optimized and may contain engineering shortcuts.

To fulfill both goals, code generation can be used. Code generation for API proxies is offered for all API description languages. Properly generated code conforms to the API description. However, the generated code is merely the "bones" of a skeleton, only the interface of the API can be generated. The generated code skeleton provides some structure and the correct interface, but the "meat", the actual implementation, has to be added manually around the skeleton. The missing code can be added with relatively low effort, since the skeleton already provides a structure.

So which implementation tasks need to be done during this phase? This needs to be decided on a case-by-case basis. If the real backends are available, they may be integrated, otherwise a simulation of the backend is used. Requests and responses of the backends need to be transformed, input and output need to be validated and security needs to be implemented and configured, just to name a few. Some implementation details can be left out at this stage, such as traffic shaping or performance optimizations.

An API prototype is always an imperfect and incomplete implementation of the API. Actually, the prototype implementation has to be incomplete, otherwise too much time has been scheduled for realizing the prototype. To maximize the learnings from prototyping, one should focus on implementing the aspects, which are most critical. For one API, the backend connection may be on the critical path, for another API, it may be a complex input validation algorithm. Focus on these critical issues and use shortcuts for the other issues to get to a testable prototype quickly. If the backend connection is not on the critical path, the prototype API does need to be connected to the real backend and a simulation of the backend is sufficient at this stage.

For simple APIs without any critical issues or the need to learn anything before implementation, one might be able to hop over the prototyping phase and go directly to the implementation phase.

3.2.4.1. Validation of Phase 3: Acceptance Tests with Pilot Consumers

API prototypes are usually built to answer the question "What are the major hurdles for building this API?" Besides exploring the feasibility, the prototype can be used for acceptance tests by pilot consumers. Let's see what this means.

In general, an acceptance test is a black-box testing method, where users test if the specifications and requirements of a system are met. Acceptance tests are used to verify the completeness of a system. In our case, API consumers test the API prototype. Ideally, they use the API when designing or building their app. In an acceptance test of the API, the consumers answer the question "Does this API provide some value for my app?"

Pilot consumers need to be API consumers, who are willing to work with unfinished APIs with changing interfaces, broken clients, frequent updates, unavailability and low performance of the API. In short: a pilot customer must be able to bear some pain. This is why pilot consumers are typically recruited from inside the organization of the API provider, for example from a department of the API provider. In some environments, pilot consumers are also called beta testers. Ideally, the pilot consumer writes an app that solves a real problem, sometimes a pilot consumer may just write a demo app for testing the API.

Why would an API provider voluntarily become an pilot consumer? The advantage for pilot consumers is early access to innovative APIs, allowing for short time-to-market of the consumer's app. This is an advantage that should not be underestimated in an ecosystem, where time-to-market has high impact on the market share.

Besides the validation by pilot consumers, the API prototype should also be checked for conformance with the API descriptions. To some extent, conformance between implementation and API description is already ensured by code generation. However, generated code may have been changed and manually added code may still need to be checked. Such a test should include JSON wellformedness checks and JSON schema validation of the results. Both of these tests can be generated from the API description. Additional tests might need to be added manually.

3.2.5. Phase 4: Implementation for Production

The implementation for production has similar constraints as the prototype implementation described in the previous section. The implementation needs to conform to the API description and needs to be delivered as quickly as possible. In addition, the API is fully integrated into the API portfolio. The goal of properly engineering software systems, is to ensure not only the correct functional aspects (see chapters 7 and 10) but also the correct non-functional aspects (see chapter 11). Some of the most important non-functional aspects of APIs are security, performance, and availability.

When an API has reached this phase of the approach, the API description has been properly designed, has gone through several feedback loops has been verified from several perspectives. The API description should thus be stable. Just as in the previous phase, the stable and verified API description is used as a blueprint for automatically generating an API implementation skeleton. Automatic code generation ensures that the implementation is consistent with the API description, and thus is consistent with all the design decisions the description embodies.

However, the generated code is merely a code skeleton. The

behavior of the API needs to be implemented manually, by filling in the gaps of the code skeleton. In the previous phase, the feasibility of the implementation has been shown, critical aspects of the implementation have already been tested and many insights have been gained. These insights are now applied during the implementation phase.

The focus of the implementation in this phase is thus, the proper engineering of the API. Proper software engineering practices need to be used. For example, common patterns should be identified, factored out into libraries, so they can be reused across the API portfolio.

The non-functional requirements for production systems are much tougher than for prototypes. The security of the API needs to be ensured. This can be achieved by choosing and enforcing adequate security mechanisms. The availability and performance of the API need to be ensured. These properties can be ensured by applying rate limitation and caching.

3.2.5.1. Verification of Phase 4: Acceptance Tests with Pilot Consumers

The set of pilot consumers typically grows as the API matures. The first group of pilot consumers used in the prototyping stage may consist of internal consumers of the API provider. As the API matures, the set of pilot consumers may evolve into a number of hand-picked API consumers.

3.2.6. Phase 5: Publish

Publishing an API does not require a lot of work, but it is a big milestone in the lifecycle of theAPI. From an organizational perspective, the responsibility of the API is transferred from the development unit to the operations unit. But most importantly, the API and its documentation become publicly available, API consumers will start building API clients and start using the API.

Publishing the API also means freezing its interface specification. After publishing, there is no agility in the development process any longer. Changes on published APIs require a traditional change management process.

For each published API, the API provider has an implicit contract with all its API consumers, which states the interface of the API. This is why once an API gets published, its interface can never change and the API needs to be maintained for a long time. Publishing an API implies a long-term commitment for maintaining it.

Publishing an API requires an appropriate documentation for consumers. It almost goes without saying that the documentation needs to be consistent with the implementation. Sometimes, however, the problem is that the implementation gets changed during maintenance or redesign, but the documentation is not updated. This can be avoided by generating both the implementation skeleton and the documentation from the same single source of truth, from the API description.

3.2.6.1. Verification of Phase 5: Study Metrics, Reports and Logs

It is the expectation for a published API that an increasing number of consumers successfully use the API. To be able to find out if and how this expectation is actually fulfilled by the API, usage of the API has to be monitored, measured and analyzed. Some of the metrics, which might be interesting in this context are: the total number of API calls per time frame, the number of API calls per consumer, and how many API calls resulted in an error vs in success. Not only quantitative analysis is relevant, but also some qualitative analysis.

Qualitative analysis includes for example understanding and

categorizing the solutions, which the API consumers build with the API. An API provider would like to discover if API consumers use the API as intended or if they use the API in new ways that were never imagined by the API provider at the outset. Which of the usage scenarios were correctly predicted and which new usage scenarios evolved? This can also be a trigger point to find out if a new version of the API is needed and to determine if it needs to be redesigned.

For a quantitative analysis, the first step is to determine the usage of the API. The second step is to determine how successful the API is in contributing to the API solution. The third step is to draw conclusions, discover patterns in the usage, compare all the APIs in the portfolio. A relevant metric is the number successful API calls, especially if compared to the number of unsuccessful API calls. Do some API consumers have trouble getting the API to work as intended? Are there lots of error messages? Analyses according to this metric could be a trigger for updating the API documentation or redesigning the API.

Metrics are not only interesting to the API provider, but also to the API consumers. They are interested in API analytics, dashboards, reports and monitoring. The performance and availability metrics such as status reports, up-time and response time should not only be available to the API provider, but also to the API consumers.

The API provider needs to continuously evaluate if the business objectives are met and if the business objectives are still up to date. Metrics allow for calculating business value and the ROI for the API provider. Metrics allow for understanding the consumers and marketing to them better. Based on the feedback gained and the insights obtained from analytics, the provider can improve the API.

Metrics based on consumer behavior are the real feedback for the success of the API. They allow for measuring if the adoption is as expected and if the revenue is as expected. Even for successful APIs, the business or market might change and require a review if the API is still adequate for the market as it is today.

3.2.7. Phase 6: Maintenance

The simple rule for API evolution is, that the externally observable behavior of an API (from the perspective of the clients) cannot be changed, once the API has been published. Already a small change of the API might break some of the clients consuming the API. It is impossible to update all the consumers or at least unrealistic, since they are under control of different owners. Thus, longevity and stability are important aspects of published APIs.

The restriction imposed by this rule might sound severe and even counter-intuitive, since APIs are often developed using an agile development approach. Agile approaches are based on feedback loops and the idea of many incremental changes of the software. The agile development approach still applies to new or unpublished APIs.

Before the publication of the API, any change can be implemented in an agile manner. As soon as the API is published, however, the game changes. When APIs are published, they become available for consumers and it has to be assumed that the consumers build apps relying on the APIs. Published APIs cannot be changed in an agile manner. At least, APIs need to stay backward- (and forward-) compatible, so that old clients do not break and new clients can use the new and improved features. See section 11.5 for details on evolution and versioning of APIs.

3.3. Discussion

3.3.1. Hand-over Points

In this approach, the contract is expressed in the form of an API description. In each phase of the approach, an API description is either created, refined or used: the API description is the red thread connecting all the steps of the approach.

When can the API description be handed over to pilot consumers? Pilot consumers need to be patient and they need to be aware of the fact that their clients might break, since the API description might still change. The earliest point in time at which a hand-over of the API description makes sense, is after the architectural and detailed design phase has been finished, the API description has been created and has been simulated successfully.

When is the API description finished? The API description is only really finished, when the API has been published, in the final phase of the approach. After publishing the API, the API description is frozen and cannot be changed without breaking potential clients.

3.3.2. Pre-Work vs. Actual Work

When you look at the proposed approach, you can see that a lot of "pre-work" is done, before the actual implementation for production starts. Is this a waste of time? No, this pre-work is required so the API is stable and does not need to be changed shortly after publication. Once an API is published, an implicit (and sometimes even explicit) contract between API provider and API consumer is made. In this contract, the API provider agrees to support the API for some time into the future, and will not make any changes that might break the client.

For the consumers this means that they can rely on the API to be around for a while and thus dare to build solutions, which rely on this API.

For the API provider, however, this contract is constraining. The API provider needs to support the API. Changes are not possible on the published API. If the API provider notices too late (i.e. after publishing) that the API should actually look and behave differently, the existing API cannot just be updated, since this would break the existing clients. Compared to this scenario, both parties are actually better off, when investing into the "pre-work" for design and verification, before beginning the "actual work" of implementation.

3.4. Summary

Many approaches for proper API design and development have been proposed and these approaches are subject of passionate debates. However, there is no wrong or right design approach, but there is an approach that fits into a specific company culture better than others.

This is why we propose that you pick and choose the phases or steps from this design and development approach that really fit your company culture. This is one of the best ways to make sure that the API design and development approach is actually adopted and lived by the team.

4. API Design with API Description Languages

API description languages are the power tools of the API designer. They make it quite easy to describe APIs in a precise manner by providing appropriate, specialized language concepts. API designers typically use API description languages to capture architectural design decisions (see chapter 5) and frontend design decisions (see chapter 7). But they are way more than that.

As we have seen in the previous chapter, API descriptions are the red thread running through all the phases of our API design and development approach: in the initial phase of API design an API description is drafted and in subsequent phases it is continuously refined, until the API is finally published.

The API description is cannot only used for the description of the API, but it can also be used for building the API with automated tool support.

In this book we introduce two API description languages: OpenAPI/Swagger (see chapter 8) and RAML (see chapter 9).

4.1. What are API Description Languages?

API description languages are domain specific languages, which are especially suited for describing APIs. They are both human readable and machine readable languages, similar to programming languages. They are intuitive languages that can be easily written, read and understood by API developers and API designers alike. API description languages are also precise, leave little room for ambiguity. They are very expressive and powerful. And they have a well-defined syntax, which makes it possible to process them automatically by software.

Compared to programming languages or API implementation languages, API description languages use a higher level of abstraction and a declarative paradigm. This means that they can be used to express the *"what"* instead of the *"how"*. For example, they define the data structure of the possible responses (the "what"), instead of describing how the response is computed (the "how").

4.2. Usage

In their short history, the role of API description languages has changed significantly. The original purpose of API description languages was the creation of API documentation, in a similar way as JavaDoc provides a language for documenting Java programs.

Today, API description languages have many additional purposes and are the *power tools* for API design. If used correctly, API description languages can serve as the *single source of truth* and as the main reference for all aspects of API design and development. API description languages are machine readable specifications of the API, that can be used for automating API development tasks and increase the productivity of API development.

In this section we present several use cases for API descriptions. These use cases are not chosen for their completeness, but they are chosen to convey the central role of API descriptions for the design and development of APIs. API descriptions are central, since they can support all phases of API design and development.

4.2.1. Communication and Documentation

Whenever APIs need to be communicated among various stakeholders, APIs needs to be described in some form. And APIs need to be communicated quite often: among API developers, between API designers and API developers and between API providers and API consumers. Because APIs need to be communicated frequently and amongst various stakeholders, it should be easy to describe APIs in a precise manner. With API description languages this can be achieved.

Since an API is an interface connecting two or more software systems, it is important that the API is understood by the involved developers on all sides. Some of the involved developers are on the side of the API provider and busy developing the API. Other developers are on the consumer side. They typically develop apps that use the API. The idea of loose coupling of services is great, as long as it is ensured that the services are well understood by the developers on API provider side and on API consumer side.

To provide a shared understanding of an API, the API needs to be well documented. This is all the more important as the developers are not co-located and can quickly share their insights. Instead, they are spread out over different companies, countries, continents and time zones. An appropriate documentation can help in this case. This is why the documentation of APIs is extremely important for both developers of the server-side API implementation and for the client-side API consumers.

Documentation is usually delivered as written prose in a document, but prose documentation may simply be not precise enough. Alternatively, some developers might consider the code sufficient as a form of documentation. A short and precise description of all the important design decisions for the API has advantages to prose documentation and to code as documentation. Code is precise but is too long, too complicated to understand, and may not be publishable due to intellectual property or security considerations.

The original purpose of API description languages is providing human readable API documentation. To relieve the developer from the burden of formatting pretty HTML pages, domain specific languages (DSL) for documenting APIs have been created. Based on such a DSL, the documentation of the API can be automatically generated. If you have used Java, you might be familiar with JavaDoc, an approach for generating documentation from specially marked annotations in Java programs. A similar approach is taken here; the documentation is generated based on a special purpose language: the API description language.

If the API documentation is written in an API description language, it has some attractive properties. The API documentation contains only relevant information and this information is available in a structured, ordered and compact form. No formatting or styling needs to be provided, but the documentation needs to follow rigid syntactic rules. In this respect, API description languages are similar to programming languages. API descriptions written in these languages are thus ideally suited for machine processing. Parsers can take the description apart and build an abstract syntax tree. This abstract syntax tree is then traversed by generators to produce other representations, for example a pretty HTML page.

While the API developer might enjoy the simplicity and clarity of the API description, the API consumer might expect the API documentation to be a pretty, colorful and interactive HTML page. To satisfy both the wishes of API provider and API consumer, a generator is used to extract the information from the API description and to generate the corresponding human-readable documentation.

API descriptions also enable the creation of an interactive documentation. Interactive documentation is not only meant to be read like regular documentation, it also includes a testing bed for the APIs. API consumers can make test calls to the real API or to a simulation of the API directly from the documentation page. They do not even have to use any external tools.

API consumers typically have a choice between alternative APIs, which roughly do the same thing. The first point of contact between API consumer and API is the documentation. A documentation, which is better than the alternatives and ideally is interactive, may convince an API consumer to choose this API over alternative APIs.

4.2.2. Design Repository

The API description of an API proxy is the central source of truth for this API. For example if you are ever in doubt, which version of the API accepts a certain parameter or which status codes are returned by the API, the API description is the definitive, authoritative point of reference. The API description contains all the important design decisions for that API proxy. Not only a single API proxy should be documented, but the complete API portfolio, including the API descriptions of all API proxies. To provide a history and synchronized access in a distributed development team, the API descriptions should be put under version control, e.g. in a GIT or SVN repository.

4.2.3. Contract Negotiation

From a process perspective the API description can serve as a design contract. This contract can be used for agreements between API designer and API developer or as a contract between API consumer and API provider. The API description enables contract-first design. Both contracting parties negotiate this contract, decide on it and rely on this contract during the implementation and maintenance phases.

Traditionally, app developers would need to wait for the implementation of a new API. Contract-first design allows starting the implementation of the app by the consumer before the provider has finished building the API. Thus contract-first design allows for a very efficient development process with a much quicker turn around time. It allows app developers to bring their apps to market quicker than before. In contract-first design, the precise description of the design contract is essential. This is the strength of API description languages.

4.2.4. API Implementation

Since the API description is machine readable, it can be used for automating tasks in software development. Such an approach follows the ideas of generative software development, model driven development and domain specific languages. If used correctly, these approaches have the potential to increase the productivity of software development.

The API description can be used by the API provider to automatically generate API skeletons. An API skeleton contains some important pieces of the implementation, it is, however, not complete. The skeleton needs to be extended and filled with manual implementation before the API can be used.

These skeletons may contribute to a higher speed of API implementation as well as to a higher quality of the API implementation. The advantage of this approach is that the developer does not need to write all the code himself; a large portion of the code is already generated for him. Another advantage is improved code quality, since the generated code is consistent with the API description.

When the first iteration of the API implementation is generated from the API description, the API implementation is created from scratch. There is no prior implementation to take care of and the API implementation initially only consists of the API skeleton.

A challenge for automated code generation are updates to the API description. If a previous implementation already exists, the newly generated code needs to be merged with the existing code. Depending on the code generation framework, this might be supported by specific code markers, which are used to separate the generated code skeleton from the API implementation.

4.2.5. Client Implementation

On the API consumer side, the API description can be used for code generation. Client stubs for accessing the API can be generated. And with an appropriate code generator, the client stub can even be generated for the programming language used by the consumer.

For the API consumer, code generation has a couple of advantages. By generating the client stub for accessing the API, it is ensured that the implementation actually matches the specified contract. In addition, code generation speeds up the development process.

But the API consumer can only enjoy these benefits if the API provider makes the API description available to the consumers. It is the responsibility of the API provider, to make the API descriptions available. One elegant possibility is that the API serves its own API description on a specific endpoint.

4.2.6. Discovery

How does the client know about the capabilities of the API? One answer is: the client does not need to know, since the API needs to be understood by the API consumer and she develops the client. The consumer can learn about the API from the human-readable documentation. Another answer is: the client needs to be able to explore or discover the capabilities of the API programmatically. With such an automated discovery mechanism, an app may include new APIs, which have not been known at design time.

To enable such an implementation, an API description of the API portfolio should be served by a specific endpoint. This allows the caller to discover each API within the portfolio by downloading and parsing the API description. A precondition is that the API provider made the API description available to the consumers.

4.2.7. Simulation

To create a simulation, a model of the real world is needed. An API description contains such a model. The API description specifies the input data in the form of query parameters, form parameters, header parameters, path parameters or a data structure of the HTTP body, so the simulation can verify input according to the specification. The API description specifies the error messages, so the simulation can produce error behavior according to the specification. The API description includes an example response, which can be served as a response by the simulated API. Sometimes an example is directly provided as part of the description, sometimes a synthetic example can be constructed based on a generic specification of the data structure.

4.3. Language Features

The API description is a technical contract between API provider and API consumer, so it is important that the designed contract is unambiguous and clear. A contract should provide clarity to all involved stakeholders and should enable simultaneous development of both the consuming and providing software components. This is why the language for expressing the contract – the API description language – needs to have the following features:

- Compactness: The contract should be as compact as possible, reduced to the necessary and the relevant aspects. Repetitions should be avoided by proper language abstractions.

- Precision: Since the API description language is used for specifying a contract, it needs to be precise and unambiguous.

- Relevance: The language constructs need to be relevant for API design and should not contain unnecessary or superfluous information.

- Support for agility: The API description language should support an agile and iterative development approach. Based on a first iteration or a rough draft of an API design, it should be possible to create a refined second iteration.

- Clarity and structure: An API description language should have a well-defined syntax, thus providing clarity and structure. In contrast, a prose description of the API tends to be unclear and ambiguous.

- Support for communication: You do not need to be a programmer to understand an API description. Architects or designers should be able to read an API description as well. The generated HTML documentation is available to an even larger audience.

- Support for quick validation: It should be possible to automate the validation of an API description.

- Intuitive: It should be possible to use the API description language without a lot of training.

Any API description language should have the properties listed above. Today, a number of API description languages are available.

The Web Application Description Language (WADL) [21] was originally created for web applications but is also used for describing APIs. However, it lacks native support for JSON Schema and native support for commonly used security schemes such as OAuth. The Web Service Description Language (WSDL) [8] is intended for the description of SOAP services. It supports RPC-style services, which exchange XML-based SOAP requests and responses. WSDL cannot be used for describing REST services, since it does neither support JSON data structures, nor API security schemes such as OAuth. WADL and WSDL have been around for a long time, their use is widespread, they can be used for API design, however, they have not been created specifically for RESTful API design and thus lack important features.

The languages OpenAPI/Swagger, RAML, API Blueprint and Mashery I/O Docs have been created specifically for RESTful API design. In chapters 8 and 9 we introduce OpenAPI/Swagger and RAML, two of the most popular languages for describing APIs.

4.4. Limitations

What are the limits of API descriptions such as OpenAPI/Swagger and RAML? With API description languages you can describe frontend design decisions and architectural design decisions. Other aspects of API design, such as the behavior of the API, design of backend connections, and the specification of non-functional properties cannot be captured and need to be described separately.

4.5. Summary

API description languages are very powerful tools for API design. Proficiency in one of the main API description languages is essential for designing APIs. Learn more about them in chapters 8 and 9, where we introduce the API description languages OpenAPI/Swagger and RAML.

5. API Architectural Design Decisions

> Simplicity is the ultimate sophistication.
>
> *Leonardo DaVinci*

Each API has an architecture – but not all architectures are equally good. A "good" architectural design of the API is the foundation for the frontend design, backend design and non-functional design. How do we know what a "good" API architecture is?

The answer is: it depends. It depends on the type of the API proxy and its responsibilities. Good API architecture uses architectural patterns and architectural styles effectively to cover the responsibilities and to achieve desirable properties.

In this chapter we will study typical requirements of APIs, including the responsibilities and desirable properties of APIs. We introduce a list of architectural patterns, which are best practice in all modern APIs. Even more important are the architectural styles, which are used to construct APIs with desirable properties. For each architectural design decision we study several alternatives and discuss their advantages and disadvantages.

5.1. Requirements for APIs

Based on the typical responsibilities of APIs, we propose a list of desirable properties, which form a benchmark for "good" API design. Armed with these requirements, we can then pick appropriate architectural patterns and architectural styles for building great APIs.

5.1.1. Responsibilities of APIs

What do APIs typically do? APIs typically do not implement any business logic. The business logic and data storage are implemented in the backend systems. What is left to be done by the API?

There are four main tasks or responsibilities that need to be fulfilled by any API. These responsibilities are also the minimum requirements for any API.

5.1.1.1. Gathering Data

APIs needs to gather data from various data sources, such as different types of databases, legacy systems or enterprise service buses. For each API it needs to be decided, which backend it should use for gathering data based on the request content or the request context. Sometimes, data from multiple backend systems needs to be requested. Towards the API consumers, the API needs to hide the backend systems used, including their technology stacks, protocols and data formats.

5.1.1.2. Structuring and Formatting Data

When the data is exposed, it needs to be structured and formatted in such a way that the data can be easily consumed and integrated by the consumer. For the input and output of the API, the perspective of the API consumer is relevant, not the perspective of the existing backend systems. The API needs to mediate between the nice, clean, simple structure and format presented to the consumer and the complicated format and structure that is often required towards the backend system.

5.1.1.3. Delivering Data

In general, APIs need to expose easily consumable data in a secure manner with the required performance. When data is delivered, the consistency of the data needs to be ensured. Appropriate delivery protocols should be used by the API, e.g. for real-time data.

5.1.1.4. Securing and Protecting

The API enables new business opportunities by opening up the IT systems of the enterprise. This not only leads to new opportunities but also to new security risks. Information could be stolen, or internal systems could be compromised. To deal with these risks, the API needs to ensure that consumers are properly authenticated and authorized to access the data via API. Moreover, the API not only needs to ensure the security of the exposed data, but also the security and availability of the API platform and - to some extent - the security and availability of the backend systems, which are used by the API. The API needs to protect the API platform and the backend systems from overload and attacks.

5.1.2. Desirable Properties of APIs

Any API needs to fulfill its responsibilities (see section 5.1.1), which are gathering, structuring, delivering and securing data. Fulfilling responsibilities is the minimum requirement for APIs, but it is not enough to make the API really great and desirable for API consumers.

Which properties does an API need to have to increase its desirability? In the following we list a number of such desirable properties.

5.1.2.1. Consumer-Centric

The frontend of the API is made for API consumers, and targeted to their needs. From the API consumer's perspective, the API should be simple, clean, clear and approachable. It is the task of the API to mediate between the simple, clean, clear and approachable format presented to the consumer and the complicated format used towards the backend system.

5.1.2.2. Simple

There should be a low barrier of entry for new API consumers. The API should be simple, so new users can get started quickly and easily. The API should be easy to learn and easy to use. The challenge is to create an API that not only looks simple, but is actually easy to use. APIs that use standards and are interoperable are usually considered simple.

Using Standards and Conventions The API should apply relevant standards and follow industry conventions. Following conventions and standards also improves the understandability of the solution.

Interoperable The API should "play well with others" and interoperate in as many scenarios as possible. Following standards, conventions and best practices improves interoperability. Another simple means for improving interoperability is hiding any implementation details.

5.1.2.3. Clean

The frontend of the API must not be convoluted with many parameters and configuration options. A clean interface has a short number of parameters, uses understandable names, and follows a naming scheme.

5.1.2.4. Clear

The API operates only on one object and does only one thing – from the API consumer's perspective. The fact that there are several steps involved on the side of the API provider is irrelevant in this context.

5.1.2.5. Approachable

It should not be a secret how to use the API, it should be easy to get started using the API. This can be achieved when the API is self-explanatory, intuitive, predictable, explorable, discoverable and well documented.

Self-Explanatory, Intuitive and Predictable The URI needs to be predictable, the parameters need to be self-explanatory and the data objects need to be easy to understand. The API is consistent with the other APIs in the portfolio.

Explorable and Discoverable An API can be explorable by API consumers. A curious API consumer can explore the API without reading the documentation. APIs should also be discoverable by machines. This requires enough machine readable information in the API and following some conventions.

Well-Documented Some consumers prefer reading a documentation of the API. For these consumers the API needs to be documented in an easily digestible form, that is fun and exciting, too.

5.1.2.6. Forgiving and Forward Compatible

The API should deliver error messages that can be understood by the consumer. If the consumer made a mistake, the API provides hints for fixing the mistakes. The API should be forward compatible by handling unexpected input in a graceful way. Instead of throwing the hands up in the air and reject the request when a small detail is incorrect, the API should deliver useful results anyway.

5.1.2.7. Secure and Compliant

The API needs to ensure that it can only be accessed by authenticated and authorized consumers. The API does not leak internal information. The API is compliant with best practices and with security regulations.

5.1.2.8. Performance, Scalable and Available

For API consumers, the performance and availability of the API are important requirements. An API with high availability creates trust with the API consumers, convincing them to use the API in the first place. An API that meets the performance requirements allows them to build responsive apps with a great end user experience. Both the API and the underlying API platform need to be scalable.

5.1.2.9. Reusable

The API should not be specific for one API consumer or one project. The API itself should be reusable, but it should also be built from reusable components. This helps to make all APIs in an API portfolio behave consistently. The reusability property is desirable for the API provider, the resulting consistency among the API portfolio is desirable for the API consumer.

5.1.2.10. Backward Compatible

An API needs to be backward compatible. Old clients need to be supported. If new features do not allow for backward compatibility, a new API or a new API version is created. Once APIs are published and used, they cannot be changed or taken away. Consumers rely on the APIs to work and to work in exactly the described manner. Even though APIs can be very well developed in an agile way, once they are published and used, all the agility has to be left behind and the given version of the API only allows for backward compatible changes.

5.1.3. Summary

How do we use this long list of desirable API properties? We can use it for evaluating the architecture of APIs or we can use it to figure out what we need to improve on the architecture, so it exhibits more desirable properties.

5.2. Architectural Patterns

An architectural pattern is a reusable solution to a common challenge in architecture. For APIs, several such architectural patterns exist: the stateless server pattern (see section 5.2.1.2), the facade pattern (see section 5.2.2) and the proxy pattern (see section 5.2.3). In the remainder of this section, we study each of these patterns in detail.

How do we know which pattern to use and whether an architectural pattern is appropriate for a specific API? Use the pattern if applying the pattern yields an API with desirable properties (see section 5.1.2).

5.2.1. Client-Server Patterns

In a client-server architecture, client and server are realized as independent components, running on independent hardware and software stacks. Client and server are loosely coupled and relatively independent. Since client and server are independent but together from a complete application, they need to agree on a mechanism for maintaining the application state.

The state can be for example a set of selections that were made on a previous web site or in a previous API call. In principle, state can be maintained on the server-side or on the client-side. For both options, we introduce a pattern in the following: a stateful server pattern for maintaining the state server-side and a stateless server for maintaining the state client-side.

Typically, the stateless server pattern is chosen for APIs. To show its properties, we contrast it in the following with a stateful server.

5.2.1.1. Stateful Server Pattern

When communicating with a stateful server, the client can assume that the state and context of the previous communication is available on the server. The server maintains the application state in a persistent state object, or a session object, which is preserved in between calls. The client merely maintains an identifier for the session. This identifier is called session ID and is used to find the corresponding application state on the server. The session ID needs to be included in all subsequent calls of the client. Including the session ID into the call ensures that the corresponding session data can be identified on the server.

5.2.1.2. Stateless Server Pattern

A stateless server does not maintain any information. State can still be used, but it is realized in a different way: the client maintains the application state. The server needs to receive all the necessary information from the client with each API call and it needs to return the updated information in the API response. The server thus ensures, that the client has all necessary information to maintain state. The client keeps the state until the next call to the server.

A disadvantage of stateless communication with this client-side form of state-maintenance is the increased network traffic and processing overhead. The data that would be in the session object in a stateful architecture, is serialized and transferred to the client as part of the response, the client deserializes and processes this information and includes the relevant information into the follow-up request.

An advantage of this pattern is the scalability, availability and performance of the solution. The capacity of the solution can be increased by adding new nodes for processing and setting up the load balancer. No server state needs to be migrated to the new nodes. For the same reason, it is equally little effort to scale the solution down by removing processing nodes.

Another advantage is the conceptual simplicity from the API consumers' perspective. No preconditions need to be fulfilled before the API call can be made.

5.2.2. Facade Pattern

The responsibility of the API is to expose easily consumable data in a secure manner. Typically, the API does not need to implement the business logic or storage of the exposed data. The API is merely a facade. The business logic is executed behind the facade in internal backend systems, which are hidden from the API consumers.

The API facade uses the principle of information hiding. Hidden behind the facade are complicated backend requests with large and complicated data structures and with meta data that is irrelevant for the consumer. Examples for such hidden backend systems are databases, SOAP services, ESBs, legacy systems, legacy or proprietary protocols, monolithic mainframes or big applications. The facade is used to selectively expose internal systems and make them accessible and consumable by app developers.

A facade consists of an interface and an implementation. To create a facade, two things need to be done:

- Design the interface that would be perfect for your consumers, based on your consumers' needs.

- Create an implementation to mediate between the interface and the backend system. The implementation enforces security, authorizes consumers, monitors usage, and shapes the traffic.

Almost all APIs apply the facade pattern, especially when APIs are used to provide access to legacy systems. An exception may be APIs without any dependencies to legacy systems. They can be found in startups and young companies. In these cases, the API does not require the facade pattern, since the business logic is implemented as part of the API.

5.2.3. Proxy Pattern

A proxy provides an interface to an original object that is not intended to be exposed directly. Calls that previously called the original object directly, need to point to the proxy object instead. The calls arriving at the proxy are forwarded to the original object. The proxy does not contain any business logic, but functions as a wrapper. The wrapper may enrich the functionality of the original object or may change the access to the original object without changing the original object directly.

APIs are typically realized as proxies to the backend systems that deliver the data. APIs provide typical proxy functionality, such as simplifying, transforming, securing and validating requests and responses. The terms API and API proxy are used interchangeably.

5.3. Architectural Styles

In general, an architectural style is a large-scale, predefined solution structure. Applying an architectural style allows for building the API quicker and more consistently than without a predefined solution structure.

In this section we study several architectural styles for communication in distributed systems. The REST style (Representational State Transfer) in section 5.3.1, the HATEOAS style (Hypermedia As The Engine Of Application State) in section 5.3.2, the RPC style (Remote Procedure Call) in section 5.3.3 and the SOAP style in section 5.3.4. We compare the approaches, show advantages and disadvantages, commonalities and differences.

APIs can be realized using any of these styles. How do we know, whether a particular architectural style is appropriate for a given API? The resulting API exposes many of the previously stated desirable properties. Most commonly, APIs are realized using the REST architectural style.

5.3.1. REST Style

REST (Representational State Transfer) is an architectural style for APIs, and as such it defines a set of architectural constraints and agreements. REST is designed to make optimal use of an HTTP-based infrastructure and the HTTP protocol. The central concept of REST is the resource, which has a uniform interface. REST imposes the following constraints:

- Use of HTTP capabilities as far as possible.

- Design of resources (nouns), not methods or operations (verbs).

- Use of the uniform interface, defined by HTTP methods, which have well-specified semantics.

- Stateless communication between client and server.

- Use of loose coupling and independence of the requests.

- Use of HTTP return codes.

- Use of media-types.

Since REST is the most commonly used architectural style for APIs, we provide a very detailed introduction to REST in chapter 6.

5.3.2. HATEOAS Style

HATEOAS is an abbreviation for Hypermedia As The Engine Of Application State. HATEOAS is an extension of REST and any of the constraints and advantages of REST also apply to HATEOAS. HATEOAS has additional constraints, allowing for more dynamic architectures. These constraints allow clients to explore any API without any a-priori knowledge of data formats or of the API itself. HATEOAS constraints are an extension of REST constraints:

- All REST principles apply.

- Resources are linked to each other. Representations of API responses contain hyperlinks pointing to other resources.

- The semantics of API responses is provided by the media-types.

Since the HATEOAS style is often used for APIs, we provide a very detailed introduction to HATEOAS in section 6.6.

5.3.3. RPC Style

RPC is an abbreviation for Remote Procedure Call. RPC is an architectural style for distributed systems. It has been around since the 1980s. Today the most widely used RPC styles are JSON-RPC and XML-RPC. Even SOAP can be considered to follow an RPC architectural style.

The central concept in RPC is the procedure. The procedures do not need to run on the local machine, but they can run on a remote machine within the distributed system. When using an RPC framework, calling a remote procedure should be as simple as calling a local procedure.

5.3.3.1. How does RPC work?

A remote procedure is invoked from a client by serializing the client's parameters and additional information into a message and sending the message to a server. The server receives the message, deserializes its content, performs the requested calculation and sends a result back to the client, using the same serialization/deserialization mechanism.

5.3.3.2. JSON-RPC

JSON-RPC [20] is used to call a single procedure on a remote machine. When serializing the request or response it uses a well-defined JSON schema for JSON-RPC. It not only defines a JSON schema for the serialization of requests and responses into JSON, but also defines the fault handling with error messages. It is currently specified in version 2.

5.3.3.3. XML-RPC

XML-RPC [36]is used to call a single procedure on a remote machine. As its name suggests, it uses XML for serializing the procedure request (`methodCall`) and response (`methodResponse`). Additionally, messages for fault handling are described. The nesting of XML allows transporting complex data structures. XML-RPC has been around since 1998 and later evolved into SOAP.

5.3.4. SOAP Style

SOAP [39]follows the RPC style and exposes procedures as central concepts (e.g. `getCustomer`). It is standardized by the W3C and is the most widely used protocol for web services. SOAP style architectures are in widespread use, however, typically only for company internal use or for services called by trusted partners.

SOAP offers bindings to a variety of transport protocols, such as HTTP, SMTP, TCP, UDP or JMS. SOAP is based on XML and actually evolved from XML-RPC. A serialized SOAP message is wrapped by an envelope containing a header with meta information, and a body with either a request, a response or a fault. Complex data structures for request and response can be described by XML schema. The interface of SOAP services is described by a dedicated, standardized language, the Web Service Description Language (WSDL) [8].

SOAP offers many extensions, for example for transferring binary data, for security, federation, trust, encryption and signing - just to name a few. Some of the extensions are standardized, while others are product-specific. These extensions are also known as WS-*.

5.3.5. Streaming Style

Most APIs use the HTTP protocol. A limitation of HTTP is one-way communication, which needs to be initiated by the client. For streaming applications this results in polling of the client, essentially asking the API on the server repeatedly: "Do you have any new information for me now? ... How about now? ... And now?" This is rather inefficient and resource intensive. For streaming applications, such as chat or real-time delivery of data, other styles and protocols are commonly used, which allow for bidirectional communication, once the channel is established.

- XMPP: The Extensible Messaging and Presence Protocol (XMPP) is a communication protocol for real time communication and instant messaging.

- WebSockets: The WebSockets protocol is used for bidirectional communication between client and API. Instead of using the traditional request-response pattern, a full-duplex, bi-directional communication pattern is used. Once the connections is initiated, both client and API can send data packages. WebSockets uses the scheme (`ws://`) for unprotected communication and the WebSocket-Secure protocol (`wss://`) for TLS secured communication.

5.4. Architectural Trade-offs

APIs can be realized using any of the presented architectural styles (REST, HATEOAS, RPC, SOAP or Streaming). Sometimes there are trade-offs with other architectural demands. Good judgement has to be used to find the optimal solution. Examples of such competing architectural demands:

- Information abstraction
- Simplicity
- Loose coupling
- Network efficiency

- Resource granularity
- Convenience for the consumer
- Convenience for the provider

In the following we compare some of the most common alternatives for API styles.

5.4.1. RPC in Comparison to REST

Not every service that is exposed over HTTP is compliant with the REST constraints. Sometimes one can find services, which are advertised as being RESTful, but in reality they follow the RPC style. In fact, there may even be a grey zone between REST and RPC, when a service implements some features of REST and some of RPC. The Richardson Maturity Model can be used for determining the degree to which services are RESTful. The following levels are defined:

- Level 0: Services use an RPC style.
- Level 1: Services expose resources. Larger services are broken down into resources.
- Level 2: Services use HTTP methods correctly. Services use HTTP infrastructure efficiently.
- Level 3: Hypermedia is used according to HATEOAS. The service is self-documenting and flexible.

According to Roy Fielding, the REST style requires level 3, which is in fact HATEOAS. However, typically people speak about REST services, even if only levels 1 or 2 are reached. REST at levels 1-2 is sometimes called "pragmatic REST".

Here are a couple of simple, practical tricks to determine if a service is not RESTful:

- If the name of the service is a verb instead of a noun, the service is likely RPC and not RESTful.

- If the name of the service to be executed is encoded in the request body, the service is likely RPC and not RESTful.

- If the back-button in the web-application does not work as expected, the service is not stateless and not RESTful.

- If the service or website does not behave as expected after turning cookies off, the service is not stateless and not RESTful.

5.4.2. HATEOAS in Comparison to REST

HATEOAS is a specialization of REST, so those two contenders have a lot of commonalities. This is why we have to look into the details to compare the two styles. For this purpose we can use the four levels of the Richardson Maturity Model:

- Level 0: Services use an RPC style.

- Level 1: Services expose resources. Larger services are broken down into resources.

- Level 2: Services use HTTP methods correctly. Services use HTTP infrastructure efficiently.

- Level 3: Hypermedia is used according to HATEOAS. The service is self-documenting and flexible.

According to the model, HATEOAS is the most mature version of REST. However, HATEOAS is not widely used in practice for a variety of reasons. Realizing a HATEOAS-based solution requires quite a large paradigm shift for the designers and way more advanced and intelligent API clients than are typically used and built today. This is why HATEOAS mainly serves as a vision for the long term development of RESTful API design.

Pragmatic REST at level 2 is the architectural style, which is most commonly used today. It strikes an attractive balance between familiarity and advantageous non-functional properties. Pragmatic REST is not as foreign to designers as HATEOAS, but still provides many benefits, such as simplicity, cache-ability, performance and statelessness.

5.4.3. SOAP in Comparison to REST

SOAP makes data available as services, for example:

```
getCustomer()
```

REST makes data available as resources, for example:

```
https://domain.com/customers/123/addresses
```

REST services are considered lightweight, SOAP services are considered heavy weight. This has two reasons. SOAP services are typically coarse-grained, and deliver comprehensive data structures. REST services are typically fine-grained and serve bite-sized data structures. SOAP messages contain a lot of meta data and only support verbose XML structures for requests and responses. Also, due to their large size, SOAP services are considered complicated for service providers and for service consumers. REST services strip their data structures down to the necessary elements.

SOAP can be bound to many protocols, including HTTP, TCP, UDP and SMTP. REST is limited to HTTP. SOAP is usually used over HTTP, however, it is not optimized for HTTP: SOAP uses the HTTP-POST method, is thus non-idempotent and does not offer any cache-ability. SOAP services do not offer visibility (e.g. if this is a reading or writing access), since no semantic information about the method can be deduced. REST is optimized for the HTTP protocol and can make full use of its caching and content-negotiation features.

SOAP is well-suited for enterprise integration, due to its rigid structure, and its security and authorization capabilities. SOAP is good for transactions or for enforcing a formal software contract between consumer and provider. SOAP is typically used for integration with enterprise partners.

REST is well-suited for APIs that are intended for wide adoption with many consumers - even outside the enterprise. Due to the relatively simple data structures and fine granularity, REST is well suited for devices with limited computing resources, such as mobile devices and for the internet of things.

5.5. Summary

Architectural design decisions are the foundation for any API design. In this chapter, we have analyzed the responsibilities of APIs, since they help us to place APIs in the overall system architecture. We have identified several desirable properties of APIs, which also form some generic architectural requirements for APIs. We have studied several architectural patterns and architectural styles for APIs. Even though several architectural styles are possible, the REST architectural style is the one that is most commonly used. This is why we describe REST in more detail in the following chapter.

6. Introduction to REST

REST (Representational State Transfer) is an architectural style [17], and as such it defines a set of architectural constraints and agreements. An API which complies with the REST constraints, is said to be RESTful.

REST is designed to make optimal use of HTTP. This is a great advantage of REST, since HTTP-based infrastructure such as servers, caches and proxies, are widely available. The success of the web – based on HTTP – provides the living proof for the scalability and longevity of HTTP-based architectures. REST uses exactly these constraints and agreements that worked so well for the web and applies them to APIs.

In this chapter we explain the concepts, principles and constraints of REST and HATEOAS, in chapter 7 we show how to apply the REST architectural style when building new APIs.

But before we get started with REST, let me clear some common misconceptions: REST is not a standard. REST is not a protocol either. REST is an architectural style consisting of architectural constraints and agreements, which are based on HTTP. In the following section we introduce HTTP as the foundation of REST.

6.1. HTTP

HTTP stands for Hypertext Transfer Protocol. HTTP version 1.1 is standardized by the W3C and IETF in RFC 7230 [15], RFC 7231 [16], RFC 7232 [14], RFC 7233 [26], RFC 7234 [32] and RFC 7235 [13]. It is an application level protocol, on layer 7 of the ISO/OSI model. Some basic HTTP terminology:

Resource A resource is an abstraction of an HTTP entity, for example a website. A resource defines the abstract syntax of the entity; the concrete expression of the resource is called representation. A resource is addressable by a URI. One can interact with a resource via the Uniform HTTP Interface. It is "uniform" because it is the same for all HTTP resources.

Representation A representation is a concrete entity, which encodes a resource in e.g. HTML, JSON or XML. A resource may be available in multiple representations, such as a JSON message and as an XML message. By decoupling resource from representation, systems may expose multiple representations per resource. The advantage is, that the right representation can be chosen based on the client's processing capabilities.

Uniform HTTP Interface All resources have the same, uniform interface, which can be used to perform operations on the resource. The Uniform HTTP Interface defines CRUD operations for creating, reading, updating and deleting resources. The CRUD operations are defined by the HTTP methods POST, GET, PUT, DELETE.

Uniform Resource Identifier (URI) A Uniform Resource Identifier (URI) is the address of the resource and identifies the resource. A URI can be either a Uniform Resource Locator (URL) or a Uniform Resource Name (URN).

6.2. REST Concepts

REST is an architectural style consisting of architectural constraints and agreements, which are based on HTTP. This is why REST uses many of the HTTP concepts introduced before.

6.2.1. Resource

Just as in HTTP, the central concept of REST is the resource. A resource is an abstract data model, which may be built hierarchically and contain sub resources. Each resource (and even sub resources) can be identified by their unique URI (Uniform Resource Identifier).

A resource is a data structure, which can be serialized to various concrete representations, such as a JSON representation or an XML representation. To create, retrieve, update or delete a resource, a number of different methods are defined. However, not each resources may support all methods.

Resources are almost like objects in the object oriented programming paradigm (OOP). This comparison holds, as far as it concerns the presence of data fields and methods, which manipulate the data fields. There is, however, one important difference between REST and OOP: The methods in REST are restricted to the set of HTTP methods (GET, PUT, POST...), whereas in OOP the methods can be arbitrary. This set of HTTP methods is the uniform resource interface. Besides the HTTP methods specified in the uniform resource interface, no other methods can be used to manipulate the resource. No other methods can be stated in API requests, neither in the HTTP body nor in the base path nor in the parameters.

6.2.2. API

The term API is not officially defined in REST. We specify an API as a root-resource, which can contain other sub resources. What is the difference between APIs and resources? Resources form hierarchical data models. In this hierarchy, the root resource is somewhat special. We call it an API. An API may contain several sub resources, which are typically used together.

6.2.3. Representation

Concrete data is served in the form of representations. Think of a representation as a serialized resource. Different encoding schemes (or media-types) can be used for serialization. Thus, each resource may come in a number of representations.

What is the difference between resources and representations? Resources are an abstract data model. As soon as a resource is returned to a client, it needs to be serialized into a concrete string representation. The rules for creating these representations may be different, producing XML or JSON, but all representations of the same resource contain the same information: the information of the resource.

6.2.4. Uniform Resource Interface

REST APIs mostly perform CRUD (create, read, update, delete) operations, which can be easily mapped to HTTP methods: creation can be performed by a POST, reading is performed by GET, updating is performed by PUT and a deletion is performed by a DELETE. These HTTP methods constitute the Uniform Resource Interface; it is the same for all resources.

Each of the HTTP methods has a specific purpose and also a specific set of characteristics: HTTP methods can be safe and idempotent. Idempotent methods may be executed repeatedly without altering the end result; executing the method multiple times has the same effect as executing the method only once. Safe methods do not have any side effects, do not change the state of the resource and are read-only.

In REST we build resource-oriented interfaces. With resource-oriented interfaces, data structures are the abstractions, and a resource model is the interface. A few fixed operations (the HTTP methods) are used to operate on the resource interfaces. An example: If you want to model a shopping cart in an e-commerce store, you would only model a `shoppingcart` resource, which defines the interface. It goes without saying that you can use the HTTP methods of the Uniform Resource Interface to create (POST), read (GET), update (PUT) and delete (DELETE) the shoppingcart.

REST is incompatible with the commonly used procedure-oriented style for SOAP or RPC web services, where procedures are first class objects. When defining procedure-oriented interfaces, activities or operations are the abstraction. Coming back to our example of the e-commerce store and its shopping cart, we would model it as follows using SOAP or RPC: `createShoppingCart()`, `updateShoppingCart(id, newItem)`, `getShoppingCart(id)` and `deleteShoppingCart(id)`.

6.3. REST Constraints

REST defines a number of constraints for API design. Many of the REST constraints are actually HTTP constraints, and REST leverages these HTTP constraints for APIs. The REST style ensures that APIs use HTTP correctly. These constraints limit the freedom of design, so not every design is allowed any more. By using HTTP correctly in APIs, you get many desirable properties "for free", see section 6.5. REST imposes the following constraints:

- Use of HTTP capabilities as far as possible.

- Design of resources (nouns), not methods or operations (verbs).
- Use of the uniform interface, defined by HTTP methods, which have well-specified semantics.
- Stateless communication between client and server.
- Use of loose coupling and independence of the requests.
- Use of HTTP return codes.
- Use of media-types.

In section 7 we show in detail, how these REST constraints can be applied for API frontend design.

6.4. State in REST

In distributed systems, information needs to be preserved in between calls. This preserved information is also called "state". Since distributed systems consist of both client and server components, the state could be preserved in either component. A component, which stores state information in between calls is called a stateful component. A component which is agnostic to state information is called a stateless component. See section 5.2.1 for more info on the concept of state in distributed systems.

According to the well-known constraints of REST (see section 6.3), the server components are stateless and all state information is stored in stateful client components. Server components are stateless in the sense that they do not store session information in between calls.

But, it is a little more complicated than that. This causes a lot of confusion about the topic of keeping state in REST. Let me give you an example: If a client POSTs an object to the server, doesn't the state of the server component change? Is it still RESTful despite the state in the server components?

The fog starts to lift, when we realize that there are in fact two types of "state" in RESTful applications: application state (see section 6.4.1) and resource state (see section 6.4.2).

6.4.1. Application State

Application state is used for keeping track of the interactions in a single instance of a client application. Application state is not shared amongst client applications, it is dedicated to one single application instance.

In many non-REST systems, application state is held in a session object on the server. The session object is created or updated as a side effect of the client calling a function on the server.

In REST systems, however, application state is only stored in client components - not in server components and thus not in the API. APIs do not maintain application state. Each API request should be independent of the previous request. This is why each request needs to contain all the necessary information. This principle of statelessness ensures that the infrastructure can be scaled easily and dynamically (and the application state will not a concern when scaling).

Since application state is managed by client applications, the API consumer needs to take care of it and it is the API consumer's responsibility to build clients according to this pattern.

6.4.2. Resource State

Resource state represents the state of a business objects, which is made available as a REST resource. It is shared by all applications and all application instances. To realize the information sharing, the only viable option is storing the resource state on the server.

It is the responsibility of the API to provide mechanisms for changing the resource state. The HTTP methods POST, PUT, PATCH and DELETE are typically used to update the resource state via an API.

6.4.3. Anti-Pattern: Using Token Attributes to Store Application State

A common anti-pattern that I see is using token attributes to store application state. The token is used as a session id on the server and custom attributes are associated with the token and stored on the server.

Don' t get me wrong, it does make sense to store a customer ID, user ID or similar identifier describing the identity of the resource owner as an OAuth token attribute directly after login. However, that is it. No application specific data should be written to the OAuth token.

Why is this an anti-pattern? The state changes in tokens are not explicit. Making state changes completely intransparent. This results in APIs, which are hard to understand, hard to use and hard to maintain.

6.4.4. Summary

In RESTful applications, application state is managed by the client and resource state is managed by the API. It should be avoided to use tokens as session objects and store application state in them.

6.5. Advantages of REST

Each of the REST constraints (see section 6.3) contributes to the desirable system properties. In return for following these constraints, designers can expect systems that have several desirable properties.

An advantage of REST is the scalability of the system. Since REST systems are stateless and the requests are independent, it is easier to scale the system by adding another server. The same features also allow for fault tolerance, and an improved availability and reliability of the complete system. Another advantage of using this architectural style is the performance of the resulting solutions. Caching functionality can be achieved for free, i.e. without any additional implementations, since it is already taken care of by existing HTTP infrastructure, such as HTTP caches.

Another advantage is the support for handling multiple content-types. An API may be able to deliver the resource in multiple, alternative representations, and the client may be able to read responses in only one of these representations. The content-type negotiation mechanisms defines how client API can exchange information about their capabilities and negotiate the appropriate content-type. This mechanism is inherited from HTTP.

Another advantage of REST is its simplicity. The creation of a new REST API does not require a lot of overhead. In comparison, the creation of SOAP services requires a larger overhead, due to the specification of WSDL files with a compatible implementation. The REST limitation to the uniform resource interface contributes to the discoverability of APIs. With some experience in HTTP, the available methods are self-explanatory, intuitive and predictable, since the same methods are used in each and every API. As a result, consumers can quickly access the service and perform calls. REST services provide visibility, since it makes the intent of a request available and accessible to any HTTP component. Roy Fielding defines visibility as the "ability of a component to monitor or mediate the interaction between two other components"[17]. HTTP ensures – when used correctly – visibility. The correct use of HTTP in APIs requires the appropriate HTTP methods and correct status codes.

6.6. HATEOAS Style

HATEOAS is an abbreviation for Hypermedia As The Engine Of Application State. It is an extension of REST or a strict interpretation of the HTTP principles for API. Any of the constraints and advantages of REST also apply to HATEOAS. HATEOAS has additional constraints, allowing for more dynamic architectures. These constraints allow clients to explore an API without any a-priori knowledge of data formats or of the API itself.

6.6.1. HATEOAS Concepts

According to HATEOAS, APIs should be self-descriptive. All actions, which can be performed on resources are described in the representations of the resources in the form of annotated links. Each resource contains links to other resources.

The annotated links can be navigated by a generic client, which can interpret and follow links. Since all resources are linked, the client only need to have access to the root resource. From there on, the client can follow the links to reach any other resource.

HATEOAS allows for defining very dynamic architectures, that can deal with change. The client always navigates to the needed resource by following links. There are no breaking changes, because the client does not need to make any assumption about the API. All meta-information needed for making the next call is obtained from the response of the previous call. If the API is changed, the resources, which link to the changed resource need to be updated with new links and new associated meta-information. This is all that is needed to make changes in this architecture.

The client does not need much a-priori knowledge about the API or its URLs. It does however need knowledge about the semantics of the resource, to be able to interpret the responses received from the API. The semantics of the resources is provided by media-types (see 7.3.2). This is why the HATEOAS style is also known as the hypermedia style.

An API following the HATEOAS style can be modeled as a state machine, consisting of states and transitions. Resources correspond to the states and the links between the resources correspond to the transitions of the state machine. A client works with this state machine by interpreting meta-information, extracting links and following them.

6.6.2. HATEOAS Constraints

HATEOAS constraints are an extension of REST constraints:

- All REST constraints apply (see section 6.3).

- Resources are linked to each other. Representations of API responses contain hyperlinks pointing to other resources.

- The semantics of API responses is provided by the media-types.

6.6.3. Advantages of HATEOAS

Following the HATEOAS constraints, allows for the following advantages:

- Flexibility: new versions, or changed media-types can be realized without breaking any clients. For example, it is in the hands of the server to transparently change the URI structure.

- Simple client logic: the client does not need any a-priori knowledge of the API or its URIs. It does need knowledge about the semantics of the media-types.

- Simple evolution of APIs: API and client do not need to evolve in synch, as they need to with REST, RPC or SOAP.

6.7. Summary

In this chapter we have introduced the REST and HATEOAS architectural styles, since they are the most commonly used architectural styles for APIs. In the following chapter on frontend design decisions, we will explain in detail how the REST and HATEOAS constraints are interpreted and applied when building new APIs.

7. API Frontend Design Decisions

The first thing we see about a new web application, is typically its user interface. This is why user-interface design is so important for web applications. The frontend of the API is what the consumer sees first when using the API. Now, user interface design is for web applications, what API frontend design is for APIs. The results of the frontend design are directly visible to the consumer of the API, who develops apps using the APIs. This is why the frontend design is said to have an effect on the developer experience (DX), in analogy to the user experience (UX) of user interfaces. In the eyes of developers, great API frontend design can turn good APIs into great APIs.

API frontend design depends on the architectural design decisions (see chapter 5) made earlier: Different design decisions have to made in the API frontend whether the API follows the RPC, SOAP or REST architectural style. In this and the following chapters, we assume that the REST architectural style is chosen, since it is the most common and most popular architectural style for APIs. With this assumption we can focus exclusively on the design of RESTful APIs.

In this chapter we explain in detail how the architectural constraints of REST can be best used and applied for designing the frontend of APIs. We thus need to design the REST concepts, such as resources (see section 7.1), URIs (see section 7.2), representations (see section 7.3), parameters (see section 7.4), methods (see section 7.5) and status codes (see section 7.6). In addition we perform input and output validation (see section 7.7), design the API frontend for intuitive use (see section 7.8) and for ease of integration (see section 7.9).

API frontend design lends itself to contract-first design. What does the contract specify? The API frontend design contract contains a specification of the endpoints, URLs, parameters, methods, the data models, data formats etc. Such a contract can be captured using API description languages (see chapter 4) such as Swagger (see chapter 8) or RAML (see chapter 9).

7.1. Resources

A resource model describes the structure of the data being served or being accepted by the API. Each API proxy has such a resource model – whether it is explicitly specified or not. Since it is hard to change the resource model later on, it is important to get it right from the beginning and invest some time in the design of the resource model.

Designing a resource model is similar to designing classes in object oriented design, with the difference that the methods of the resources are already predefined by the HTTP methods.

When designing a resource model, lots of questions need to be answered. What should the scope of the resource be? Which attributes does it have? What is included and what not? How can the relationship to other resources be described? How can collections of resources be modeled? In this section we tackle these questions and show how to slice the problem to get an appropriate resource model.

7.1.1. What is a Resource?

A resource is a data structure that is uniquely identifiable by its Uniform Resource Identifier (URI). Think of a resource as a row in a database table which can be identified by a key. The resource just contains the raw data of the business object, it does not specify how the data has to be represented or serialized – the same is true for the data in a row of a database table. Different representations or serializations of the same resource or database row are possible: as text, PDF, XML or JSON. The structure of the resource is defined by a resource type, just as a row in the database table is defined by the schema of the database table. Since resources are directly addressable, it is possible to create links from one resource to another. In databases this is usually accomplished by foreign keys.

We can differentiate three categories of resources: collection resources, instance resources and controller resources.

A collection resource is a list of other resources. All the resources in a collection resource are of the same type. An example for a collection resource is a list of customers.

```
{
        "customers": [
                {
                        "firstname":"Tom",
                        "lastname":"Smith",
                        "id":"123"
                },
                {
                        "firstname":"Mike",
                        "lastname":"Brown",
                        "id":"456"
                }
        ]
}
```

It is available at the URL:

```
https://domain.com/customers
```

An instance resource represents a single business object. Typically, all instance resources of a certain type are grouped into a collection resource. An instance resource is for example a certain customer with ID 123.

```
{
        "firstname": "Tom",
        "lastname": "Smith",
        "id":"123"
}
```

103

It is available at the URL:

```
https://domain.com/customers/123
```

A controller resource represents a long running process. An example would be a batch process for duplicate removal in the list of customers. It is available at the URL:

```
https://domain.com/customers/duplicateRemoval
```

In the following sections, each resource category is described in detail.

7.1.2. Instance Resources

The resource available at the URL

```
https://domain.com/customers/123
```

is an instance resource and delivers data of a specific customer. The URL for the resource consists of a plural noun (customers) and an identifier of the instance (123).

The resource holds the data for a specific business object, here the customer, consisting of `firstname`, `lastname` and id.

```
{
    "firstname": "Tom",
    "lastname": "Smith",
    "id":"123"
}
```

What is the identifier used in the frontend? The identifier, here 123, can be a key that is exclusively used for the frontend or it can be the key that is also used by the backend system delivering the data. In some situations it might be ok to reuse the key from the backend system on the API frontend, but not in all cases. You need to be aware that the key becomes visible. Watch out that you do not leak any additional information by exposing the key. By studying the key, attackers might be able to guess other keys and thus gain access to data that they are not supposed to access. So if it is easy to guess other keys and the data needs to be protected, you need to translate between a random instance resource identifier used in the frontend API and the key to the data in the backend.

7.1.3. Collection Resources

Usually, there is not only a single instance resource in a system, but there are several instance resources of the same resource type. Collection resources offer a container to manage all the resources of the same type. It is a convention to choose a plural noun as the name of the collection resource. An example for a collection resource is a list of customers. The collection is available at

```
https://domain.com/customers
```

Individual customers are sub resources of the collection resource, for example available at

```
https://domain.com/customers/123
```

All sub resources that are part of a collection should have the same resource type. This restriction makes it easy for the client to iterate over the collection.

The access to collection resources typically contains modifiers, e.g. to filter resources with specific properties, to sort the resources, to group similar resources or to search for resources with specific properties. If no matching resources are found with filtering or searching, an empty collection is returned. This example searches the collection for all customers with first name Tom.

```
GET https://domain.com/customers?firstname=Tom
```

A collection resource can also be used as a factory for creating new resources (see Factory Pattern [18]). A POST request is sent to the URL of the collection resource to create a new instance resource and add it to the collection. The values for the new resource are sent as form parameters. The response is a 201 status code, indicating the creation of the resource and a Location header with the address of the newly created resource.

```
POST https://domain.com/customers
firstname=Tom&lastname=Smith
-> 201 Created
Location: https://domain.com/customers/123
```

7.1.4. Controller Resources

In RESTful design, resources are first class citizens. Custom methods are not explicitly designed, instead the standard methods of HTTP (GET, PUT, POST, ...) are used. Sometimes, no sensible resource and standard HTTP method can be identified to describe a desired functionality. For example for triggering a batch process. Batch processes are typically long-running processes that run asynchronously.

In this case, the functionality is modeled as a controller resource. It is triggered by a POST to the controller resource, which returns a status code `202 Accepted`. This merely indicates that the process is submitted. Via location header in the response, the address of a newly created status resource is returned to the client.

```
POST https://domain.com/customers/duplicateRemoval
-> 202 Accepted
Location: https://domain.com/customers/duplicateRemoval/502034
```

The status resource allows the client to track the status of the process. The status resource should include fields such as current status and the estimated execution time of the process. The status of the long running process can be obtained by a GET on the status resource, usually by client-side polling. To make polling more efficient, the API can include a recommendation for the polling interval in the status representation.

On completion of the process: Return status `303 See Other`

with a URL in the Location Header, pointing to the result produced by the process.

```
GET https://domain.com/customers/duplicateRemoval/502034
-> 303 See Other
Location: https://domain.com/customers
```

On failure: Return 200 OK with an updated process resource, indicating the failure.

```
GET https://domain.com/customers/duplicateRemoval/502034
-> 200 OK
{
        "error":"concurrent access"
}
```

Processing: Return 200 Ok with an updated process resource.

```
GET https://domain.com/customers/duplicateRemoval/502034
-> 200 OK
{
        "progress":"20%",
        "estimated_time_to_completion":"5 min 4 sec"
        "polling_intervall":"20 sec"
}
```

An asynchronous delete can be implemented in a similar fashion via a control resource, except that the completion case does not return status code 303, but status code 200.

7.1.5. Resource Ordering

Resources can be built hierarchically. In this hierarchy, a resource may be subordinated to another resource. As a result, the resource model forms a tree. In this tree, a resource can be either a root resource or a sub resource. The ordering[1] of the resources is expressed in the URL[2] of the resources.

7.1.5.1. Root Resource

A root resource (sometimes also called top resource) is the resource at the root of the tree. For example:

---

[1] Note that resource ordering is not the same as containment of resources. Resource relations are discussed in section 7.1.7.

[2] URL design is discussed in section 7.2.

107

```
https://domain.com/customers
```

7.1.5.2. Sub Resource

A sub resource is subordinated to another resource. Sub resources can be addressed directly via a separate URI. This separate URI is constructed by appending a URI fragment to the URI of the root resource. An example: A sub resource of customers is a specific customer with identifier 123 and a sub resource of that are the addresses of the customer. For example:

```
https://domain.com/customers/123/addresses
```

7.1.6. Resource Granularity

Resource design needs to find answers to the questions: How big should the resource be? How many fields should the resource contain? In finding answers to these questions, at least two perspectives need to be considered:

- From the perspective of the API provider, the chosen granularity should optimize the reusability of the resource.

- From the perspective of the API consumer, the chosen granularity should optimize (1) the simplicity, understandability and usability of the API as well as (2) the performance of the API. Any superfluous elements in the resource model should be avoided – but all the necessary elements should be included.

This is a balancing act, as the requirements for reusability and minimization are not easily reconciled. In any case, the granularity of existing data structures of backend services or database tables should not be a criterion in the granularity discussion. The data structures offered by existing backends or services were designed for internal consumption – not for consumption by consumers. These backends and services are usually too big, too complex and cannot necessarily be understood intuitively by consumers.

If in doubt, look at the resource granularity from the perspective of the consumer. Orient your design around the needs and the understanding of your consumers not around your internal data model. Data fields used for internal housekeeping in the backend should definitely not be included.

Choosing the right resource granularity is important for optimizing efficiency: If the resource is too big and contains data that is not needed, bandwidth is wasted. If the resource is too small, several requests to related resources have to be placed by the client, leading to inefficiency due to a relatively high protocol overhead for each request.

What can be done to change the size of the resource? You can split a bigger resource into multiple smaller resources and link them. Or you can merge several small and related resources into a bigger one. These changes should preserve the relation among the involved resources. We explore the alternatives in section 7.1.7.

7.1.7. Resource Relations

Resources are usually not isolated, but they are related to other resources. Here we show different options for modeling these relations to other resources.

Let's start with an example. In this example the relation between customer 123 and the messages she receives (message 456 and message 789) are modeled.

7.1.7.1. Option 1: Resource Ordering

This option expresses the messages as a sub resource of the customers resource. The messages resource is a collection resource. It returns the list of message IDs. Each message is a sub resource of messages.

```
GET https://domain.com/customers/123
-> 200 OK
{
        "name": "hans"
}
```

```
GET https://domain.com/customers/123/messages
-> 200 OK
{
        "messages": [456,789]
}
```

```
GET https://domain.com/customers/123/messages/456
-> 200 OK
{
        "from":"hans",
        "to":"hugo",
        "subject":"info"
}
```

This option is limited to a expressing hierarchical, tree-like data structures. For example, it is not easy to express links between messages of different customers. The nesting depth might get deep quickly and the URL will get longer and unreadable.

7.1.7.2. Option 2: IDs and Separate Root Resources

The customer resource contains a list of IDs. Each of these IDs corresponds to a message-resource of the respective customer.

```
GET https://domain.com/customers/123
-> 200 OK
{
        "name": "hans",
        "messages": [456,789]
}
```

```
GET https://domain.com/messages/456
-> 200 OK
{
        "from":"hans",
        "to":"hugo",
```

```
        "subject":"info"
}
```

```
GET https://domain.com/messages/789
-> 200 OK
{
        "from":"hugo",
        "to":"hans",
        "subject":"Re-info"
}
```

The consumer needs to know how to interpret the message IDs, she especially needs to know that the URL of the messages can be constructed by appending the ID to the base path:

```
https://domain.com/messages/
```

To be able to interpret and navigate the data structure, the consumer will need to be tightly coupled to the resource model of the API. This option does not impose any limits of a hierarchical tree-like data structure. It allows for representing arbitrary graphs. The same message could be referenced from two different customer resources without replicating it. This is possible in Option 2, but would not have been possible in Option 1. Use Option 2 to save bandwidth and when API consumer and API provider are tightly coupled or identical.

7.1.7.3. Option 3: Links and Separate Root Resources

Option 3 includes a full link between the customer resource and the message resources, instead of just IDs as in Option 2. As a result, Option 3 conforms to the HATEOAS style.

```
GET https://domain.com/customers/123
-> 200 OK
{
        "name": "hans",
        "messages": [
                {
                        "href":"https://domain.com/messages/456"
                        "rel: "messages",
                        "method: "GET",
                        "media-type: "application/json"
                },
                {
                        "url":"https://domain.com/messages/789"
                        "rel: "messages",
```

111

```
            "method": "GET",
            "media-type": "application/json"
        }
    ]
}
```

```
GET https://domain.com/messages/456
-> 200 OK
{
        "from":"hans",
        "to":"hugo",
        "subject":"info"
}
```

```
https://domain.com/messages/789
-> 200 OK
{
        "from":"hugo",
        "to":"hans",
        "subject":"Re-info"
}
```

The advantage is that the consumer does not need to know anything specific about the resources, how to interpret the message ID, or how to construct a URL for retrieving the message. The consumer just has to know how to follow links; a knowledge that is generic and independent of a particular resource, especially if standards are applied for modeling resource links. See section 7.1.8 for a detailed recommendation on modeling resource links.

Use Option 3 if API consumer and API provider should be loosely coupled and independent.

7.1.7.4. Option 4: Embedded Resources

In Option 4 we have merged all resources into a single resource for customer 123. There are no separate resources for the messages.

```
GET https://domain.com/customers/123
-> 200 OK
{
        "name": "hans",
        "messages": [
                {
                        "from":"hans",
                        "to":"hugo",
                        "subject":"info"
```

```
            },
            {
                "from":"hugo",
                "to":"hans",
                "subject":"Re-info"
            }
        ]
}
```

A limitation of Option 4 is, that it can only be used for expressing hierarchical resource relations (trees). Arbitrary graphs can not be modeled by embedding.

An advantage of embedding is the high performance that can be achieved. Use this option if it is a common request pattern of the clients to get all message resources whenever they access the customer resource. For this specific request pattern a single embedded resource a higher performance can be achieved than for any of the other options.

7.1.7.5. Option 5: Combinations

In this section we have introduced four options for modeling resource relations. In real life, we combine the different options. Some relations may be modeled as embedded resources (see section 7.1.7.4), while other are links (see section 7.1.7.3), IDs (see section 7.1.7.2), or subordination (see section 7.1.7.1).

7.1.8. Resource Links

You have decided to use links for modeling the relation between two or more resources (Option 3 in the previous section 7.1.7.3). So how should the links be expressed?

A link should contains not only the URL, but all the information necessary to make a call, such as the HTTP method to be used and some meta-description of the relationship between the source of the link (current resource) and the target of the link (resource we link to). Following IETF RFC 5988 [29], a link should consist of the following:

113

- A target URL pointing to the target resource (field `href` in the example).

- A relation type, providing the semantics or meaning of the relation. A basic set of relation types is already defined in the standard, such as `next` or `previous` (field `ref` in the example).

- Optionally, a context URI, identifying ing a frame or context in which this link is used. For example if the link is used in the resource of a certain web application, the context URI may point to the web application.

- Optionally, one or several target attributes. Target attributes could be the name of the link, a field for the media-type (field `media-type` in the example), a field for the HTTP method (field `method` in the example) or fields for parameters (field `parameters` in the example) .

An example of a link to a customer:

```
{
    "href": "https://domain.com/customers/1234",
        "rel": "customers",
    "method": "GET",
    "media-type": "application/json",
    "parameters": {
        "active": true
    }
}
```

7.1.9. Best Practices for Resource Design

Resource models should not contain redundant data, should not expose internal data or composite resources.

7.1.9.1. No Redundancy

When designing a resource model you should avoid data redundancy. Oftentimes this can be achieved by linking two resources instead of serving the same data in several resources.

7.1.9.2. No Internal Data

When designing your data model based on an existing internal data structure or database schema, take care not to expose any internal implementation details. This is why your resource data model should not be a 1:1 mapping of the data in the data base, but a filtering or a projection.

7.1.9.3. No Composite Resources

Composite resources are offered by some APIs for convenience of the consumer or for performance optimizations of certain use cases. Composite resources actually combine and merge several resources. Embedding is used to model the resource relation (see section 7.1.7.4). With a composite resource, the consumer only needs to perform one single request instead of several requests.

Composite resources usually create problems when the API evolves. Composite resources often lead to data redundancy. They add an additional level of complexity that should be avoided if possible.

7.2. URI Design

> Cool URIs don't change.
>
> *Tim Berners-Lee*

An API is realized as a resource, and can thus be addressed by its URI. Resource design (see section 7.1) and URI design are closely linked. The URI is the Uniform Resource Identifier and its format is standardized according to IETF RFC 3986 [27]. The standard defines two types of URIs: URIs can be used as a name, then they are called URNs - Uniform Resource Names. URIs can also be used as a locator, then they are called URLs - Uniform Resource Locators.

URI and URL are often used interchangeably. But strictly speaking, URI is the more generic term, and URL is the most used and most popular term.

7.2.1. Introduction

Everyone knows what URIs or URLs are, so the introduction here is merely to establish a terminology for the following discussions. Let's study the components of this example URI:

```
https://www.domain.com:80/user/profiles?lastname=Smith&firstname=John
```

This example URI and other URIs consist of the following components:

- Protocol (or scheme), e.g. `https`
- Host, e.g. `www.domain.com`
- Port number, e.g. 80
- Path (consists of fragments), e.g. `/user/profiles`
- Query parameters, e.g. `?lastname=Smith&firstname=John`

URIs contain special characters to separate the components, making URIs easy to parse:

- `://` to separate protocol from host
- `:` to separate host from port
- `/` for hierarchies of resources in the path
- `,` or `;` for non-hierarchical resources in the path
- `-` or `_` is used for structuring long resource names and to improve their readability in the path
- `?` to separate the path from first query parameter

- & to separate the query parameters from each other

- . to separate the path from file extensions, often used for different representations, e,g, `.json` or `.xml`

URIs are case sensitive, only the scheme and the domain name are case insensitive. Ideally, all URI components should be lower case.

7.2.2. Recommendations

In the following I have some recommendations for the URIs. Do use:

- The URI uses only lower case characters. No camelCase or other use of capitals.

- URIs do not have a slash ("/") as the last character.

- Use hyphens ("-") to separate words and enhance readability. Do not use underscores ("_").

- The URI does not contain any file extension.

- Resource names in the URI are plural nouns.

Do not use:

- Blanks: blanks are allowed according to IETF RFC 3986, but in practice they do confuse some clients. This is because form encoding and url encoding apply different rules (e.g. for blanks)

- Capital characters or camelCase: URLs are case-sensitive (except for protocol and host) according to IETF RFC 3986, but some clients cannot deal with it.

117

7.2.3. URI Template

```
/{version}/{namespace}/{resource}/{resource-id}/{sub-resource}/{sub-resource-id}
```

A typical URI contains

- The version of the API, typically only the major version number is used in the path parameter, prefixed by a v, e.g. /v2

- A namespace (which is a clustering of the APIs - based on the customer perspective)

- The accessed resource in the namespace (which is typically a collection resource – using a plural noun)

- The selected resource-id

- Multiple levels of sub resources and their respective resource-ids

7.2.4. Stable URIs

The URI of an API is a part of the API signature. Any incompatible changes in the API signature, such as a different the URI, would break the clients. Thus the URI of published APIs should not change. URIs should be stable and be kept unchanged for a long time.

What should be done, when a URI needs to be changed? If URIs are changed, a permanent redirect should be initialized, using status code 301 Moved Permanently and with the new URI in the location header. Intelligent API clients have the possibility to follow redirects and seamlessly use the API under the new URI. Some additional guidance for good style on URI management can be found on the W3C webpage [1].

7.2.5. Nesting Depth

For practical reasons, the nesting depth of the path should be limited to 2-3 levels. The reason for this limitation is not a technical limitation of URIs, but a usability recommendation. Deeply nested URIs are difficult to read and understand.

An example of a URI, which does not keep this limitation:

```
GET https://domain.com/users/123/products/1254/configuration/12
-> 200 OK
{"login": "automatic"}
```

This deeply nested URI can be expressed by 3 separate APIs, which are linked by delivering IDs in the response body:

```
GET https://domain.com/users/123
-> 200 OK
{"username":"Peter"; "products":[1254, 2679]}
```

```
GET https://domain.com/products/1254
-> 200 OK
{"productname":"EMail"; "properties":[12, 13, 15, 26]}
```

```
GET https://domain.com/properties/12
-> 200 OK
{"login":"automatic"}
```

7.2.6. Maximum Length of URIs

The length of a URI is not limited according to the HTTP standard. However, there are practical limitations: some server and some browser implementations can only process URIs of up to 2000 characters.

If the length of a URI gets close to this practical limit, it is recommended to redesign the API. There are two simple approaches for this type of redesign:

1. Instead of keeping input data in the URI, it can be placed in the HTTP body.

2. Another way around this limit is the use of POST instead of GET. The parameters of a POST are placed in

119

the HTTP body and not into the URI. A disadvantage of this approach is that the usage of POST declares an unsafe and not-idempotent API, thus limiting for example the cacheability of the API.

In case the API receives a URI that is longer than the limit that can be processed by the API, the API should return status code `414 Request-URI Too Long`.

7.2.7. URLs of Collections Resources

The URL of a collection resource should contains a plural noun. So, for example the URL of the collection resource containing customer resources could be

```
https://domain.com/customers
```

The URI of instances in the customers collection could be

```
https://domain.com/customers/123
```

7.2.8. Relative URLs vs. Absolute URLs

Both absolute and relative URLs can be used. Absolute URLs contain all components of the URL (protocol, hostname, fragment...), whereas relative URLs are usually URLs without the hostname and protocol. How much of the fragment is included varies. It depends on the basis, which the relative URL is relative to.

- The URL could be relative to the hostname.

- The URL could be relative to the base path (= URL of the root resource of the API).

- The URL could be relative to the URL of the source resource, i.e. the resource that includes the relative URL as a link (see section 7.1.8).

Relative URLs have an advantage for the API provider: The API does not need to be changed, when the API is deployed onto a new machine with a new domain name. This is because relative URLs are independent of the machine, the API is running on. A disadvantage for the client is, that the relative URLs used in links first need to be resolved into an absolute URL. There are several possibilities for resolving relative URLs into absolute ones.

Absolute URLs have an advantage for the API consumer: The API consumer can just follow the links that are served by the API. The API consumer does not need to have any specific knowledge on how to resolve the URL and does not need to construct the absolute URL first.

7.3. Representations

A representation is a serialization of a resource. A resource is merely raw data. For transferring the resource between API and client, it first needs to be serialized. Representations are such serializations of resources that can are transmitted between API and client. To serialize the resource into a representation and to deserialize the representation back into a resource, a set of serialization rules is used. In HTTP, the MIME-Types can be used as serialization rules. Typical serialization rules for representations are JSON (see section 7.3.7) or XML.

7.3.1. Where can Representations be Found?

When the representation is sent via HTTP, it can be found in the HTTP body of request and response. For the various HTTP methods (see section C), the representations may be found in different places. The GET method returns representations in the HTTP body of the response. The POST and PUT methods accept representations in the HTTP body of the request and may even send representations in the response.

> Recommendation: For a given resource and representation, use it consistently everywhere - whether it is in a GET, PUT or POST method and whether it is in a request or response body.

7.3.2. Content-Type of Representations

When the representation is sent via HTTP, it can be found in the HTTP body of request and response (see section 7.3.1). In the HTTP header, the serialization rules are specified that were used for creating the representation, which can be found in the HTTP body. The HTTP header field `Content-Type` is used for specifying the serialization rules. For a JSON representation, the `Content-Type` header would have the value `application/json`.

The serialization rules are specified according to a standard called Multipurpose Internet Mail Extensions (MIME), specified in IETF RFC 2045 [4]. The serialization rules, specified according to the MIME standard are called MIME-types. A large catalog of MIME-types is maintained by IANA [24]. It contains the most common serialization rules. In addition, custom MIME-types can be defined, for example:

```
application/json;vnd.domain.customers.json+v1
```

This content-type specifies JSON (`application/json`), the JSON Schema (`vnd.domain.customers.json`) and the version (`v1`). If you need to define your custom MIME-type and want to make it publicly available, follow IETF RFC 6838 [25].

> Recommendation: Rely on standardized MIME-types if available.

7.3.3. Addressing Representations

The resource is identified by its URL. How can we address a representation of a certain resource? The separation between resource and representation allows for the support of multiple representations per resource. In fact, many APIs offer multiple representations (XML and JSON) and thus provide clients the option to chose an appropriate representation.

The primitive form of addressing representations (see section 7.3.3.1) uses separate URLs for the various representations offered. The sophisticated form of addressing representations (see section 7.3.3.2) uses the same URL for all representations in addition to an HTTP header.

7.3.3.1. Primitive Addressing of Representations

The primitive addressing of representations simply uses one URL per representation, so there is a simple 1:1 relation between URL and representation. The client can use one URL for one representation and another URL for another representation.

How to create URLs for the different representations? This can be implemented in one of various forms. We exemplify these forms for the following case: The API (`https://domain.com/api`) should support the two languages: english and german.

- Two sub resources are created, one for each language. This results in:
    - `https://domain.com/api/en`
    - `https://domain.com/api/de`

- Two different resource extensions are used:
    - `https://domain.com/api.en`
    - `https://domain.com/api.de`

- Two different query parameters are used:
    - https://domain.com/api?lang=en
    - https://domain.com/api?lang=de
- Two different subdomains are used:
    - https://en.domain.com/api
    - https://de.domain.com/api

7.3.3.2. Sophisticated Addressing of Representations

The resource is identified by its URL, the representation is identified both by the URL of the corresponding resource and in addition by the content-type (e.g. application/json) of the representation. The client can request its desired content-type for the representation via the HTTP header field Accept from the API (see section 7.3.4).

HTTP offers a mechanism for negotiating a content-type between client and API, which is both offered by the API and processed by the client. The mechanism is called content negotiation (see section 7.3.4).

> Recommendation: Use the sophisticated form of addressing representations, as it allows for the use of the HTTP content negotiation mechanism.

7.3.4. Content Negotiation

Content negotiation assumes that the sophisticated form of addressing representations is used: the same URL serves different representations, using HTTP headers to indicate the desired representation.

An API might offer a resource in several representations (r1, r2 and r3). The client receiving the representation might only be able to process certain representations (r2, r3 and r4). How can the API find a representation, that the API is capable of producing and the client is able to process?

Content negotiation is a mechanism – implemented in the API, which selects an optimal representation for the given client-preferences and API-capabilities. In the above example these would be r2 and r3.

Content negotiation takes into consideration, what the client can process and what the API can produce. The client sends his preferred representations as a weighted list via the `Accept` header to the API. An example:

```
Accept: text/html; q=1.0, text/*; q=0.8, image/jpeg; q=0.6, */*; q=0.1
```

In the `Accept` header the client specifies the alternative content-types that can be accepted and their respective priorities. In the example, the acceptable alternatives are `text/html`, `text/*` and `image/jpeg`. The priority for these alternatives can be indicated by the parameter `q`, which is stated behind the alternative it refers to. The priority can have a value between 0.0 and 1.0. The value 0.0 indicates that the respective option is not accepted and the value 1.0 indicates that the option is preferred. If q is not set explicitly, its value is 1.0 by default. A value in between 0.0 and 1.0 can be used to indicate a relative order of priorities.

Present the alternative content-types in decreasing order of priority. Some API implementations may ignore the priority specified in the q value and take the first matching content-type (reading left to right).

Wildcards (*) can be used for content-types. For example, to indicate that no other than the explicitly given choices are accepted, the client would specify `*; q=0.0`.

If the API returns an response in a representation which was determined by content negotiation, the `Vary` HTTP header field is set in the response. It indicates to caches that this is just one of several representations that can be returned for this URL. The value of the HTTP header `Vary` is a list of the factors that influenced content negotiation. These are either the `Accept` headers or * for any other information used. An example for the `Vary` response header, indicating the content negotiation was used and that the response was selected based on the client preferences in the `Accept` header.

```
Vary: Accept
```

If the content negotiation mechanism cannot find a representation, which is both accepted by the client and can be delivered by the API, an HTTP status code `406 Not Acceptable` should be returned. In the payload a detailed description of the error message should be returned. See the section on HTTP status codes and on error handling.

The same mechanism for content negotiation can be used to negotiate content types (see section 7.3.4.1), languages (see section 7.3.4.2), character encodings (see section 7.3.4.3) and content encodings (see section 7.3.4.4).

7.3.4.1. Negotiating Content-Types

As seen before, the client sends a list of preferred content-types via the `Accept` header. An example:

```
Accept: text/html; q=1.0, text/*; q=0.8, image/jpeg; q=0.6, */*; q=0.1
```

The client prefers to receive the resource as an HTML document. If not available he accepts any other form of text. If not available he accepts the resource as a JPEG image. If not available he accepts any other content-type that the API can provide.

7.3.4.2. Negotiating Language

Let's have a look at an example for negotiating the language:

```
Accept-Language: de; q=1.0, en; q=0.5
```

In this case, the client is requesting a response in German (de) and if it is not available, a response in English (en) is acceptable. Typical options for the Accept-Language header are en, de, es. If the API cannot offer a response in any of the acceptable languages, the default language of the API is returned.

7.3.4.3. Negotiating Character Encoding

The following example shows a header for negotiating character encoding:

```
Accept-Charset: UTF-8
```

Typical options are UTF-8 or US-ASCII. The default encoding for most MIME-types is UTF-8. The default encoding for the text/xml media-type is US-ASCII.

7.3.4.4. Negotiating Content Encoding

Content Encoding is actually compression. Let's have a look at an example:

```
Accept-Encoding: deflate
```

Typical options are gzip, deflate, compress. The default is no compression. If the API cannot offer a response with the acceptable compression, no compression is used.

7.3.5. Data Size of Representations

The size of the representation in bytes is determined by the size of the resource, but also by the serialization rules of the specific representation. Different representations for the same resource may result in different data sizes. XML representations, for example, typically have a larger data size than corresponding JSON representations.

In addition, the inclusion of whitespace has an impact on the data size of the representation. Pretty-printing XML structures or JSON structures will add whitespace to the representation. It improves the readability, but at the same time, it increases the data size. Since white space is repetitive, the additional size can be reduced using HTTP compression (see section 11.2.4). Thus the actual impact on the data size is low (11.2.5), and readability is more important.

7.3.6. Binary Data

Sometimes the representation contains binary data. We differentiate small binary data elements and large binary data.

7.3.6.1. Small Binary Data Elements

For small binary data elements (such as a public key for encryption) you can mix meta data and binary data in the same representation. You should use base64 encoding for the field that contains the binary data. In the following example, binary data is transferred together with non-binary data via form parameters.

```
POST https://domain.com/api/users/123/publickeys
size=2048&publickey=<base64 encoded binary data>
Content-Type: application/x-www-form-encoded
-> 201 Created
```

7.3.6.2. Large Binary Data

For large binary data (such as a video file) it is recommended to separate the meta data from the binary data. Create separate resources for binary data and metadata; do not mix them. You should, however, link from the metadata to the binary data. To identify the binary data, you can generate a UUID on the client side, use it as an identifier, build up a URL and post the binary payload to the URL. When posting the binary data, use the content-type **multipart/form-data**, as this is the default content-type for file uploads typically used by web browsers.

```
POST https://domain.com/api/data/E130C205-2CB7-4834-A359-FA250E19EFC4
<binary data here>
Content-Type: multipart/form-data
-> 201 Created
```

You create the metadata with a separate POST request and send a JSON object using the content-type `application/json`. The JSON object contains a link to the binary data.

```
POST https://domain.com/api/archive/videos
{
  "description": "Surveillance Video Cash Register 2016-09-30",
  "filename": "surveillance-2016-09-30.mp4",
  "filesize": 6723529202,
  "href": "https://domain.com/api/data/
           E130C205-2CB7-4834-A359-FA250E19EFC4"
}
Content-Type: application/json
-> 201 Created
```

The advantage of this approach is, that the resource with the raw binary data could be uploaded directly from the browser and can be loaded and shown directly in the browser. For leading and showing the data, the API needs to set the content-type header appropriately (see section 7.3.2).

The disadvantage of the approach with two resources is the potential for inconsistencies between the two resources.

7.3.7. JSON

JSON stands for the JavaScript Object Notation and is used for the serialization of objects in JavaScript, supporting hierarchical data structures and lists. JSON is standardized in IETF RFC 7159 [7]. It can conveniently be used with JavaScript, both for serialization and for deserialization. Nowadays, JSON can actually be considered a programming language independent format and libraries for JSON serialization and deserialization are available for all major programming languages.

Compared to XML, JSON is encoded more space-efficiently, leading to a lower data size (in bytes). Instead of closing tags, simple closing brackets are used. For the same reason, it can also be argued that human readability of JSON is better than XML.

7.3.7.1. JSON Schema

The structure (or schema) of JSON objects can be defined in a standardized way, in JSON Schema. It is defined as an IETF Draft [10]. For describing the structure of JSON objects, JSON Schema conveniently uses JSON syntax as well. JSON Schema supports all the structuring possibilities of JSON, such as lists, objects and primitive data types.

- Root elements in JSON can be either lists or objects.

- Objects consist of key-value pairs, values can be primitive types, lists or other objects.

- Lists are a sequence of objects, a sequence of lists or a sequence of primitive data types.

The names of data fields in JavaScript are typically camelCase, so it makes sense to use this convention in JSON as well. Since JSON is used in other programming languages as well, the use of other naming patterns, such as snake_case or PascalCase can be observed.

From my perspective, consistent naming in the API would be more important than slavishly following JavaScript conventions. See also section 7.8.1 on this topic.

7.3.7.2. JSON to XML and back again

Conversions between JSON and XML typically need to be performed in enterprise scenarios, since JSON is offered towards consumers and XML is provided by backend systems. See section 10.2.2.3for more details on this topic.

7.3.7.3. Common JSON Anti Patterns

Using JSON is not always straightforward. From experience we have collected a list of cases, where JSON has been used in the wrong way. Watch out for these common JSON Anti Patterns.

Serialization and Deserialization in JavaScript JavaScript offers the built-in method `JSON.stringify()` for serialization of a JavaScript object to a JSON string. It also offers the built-in method `JSON.parse()` for deserialization of a JSON string to a JavaScript object. JavaScript also offers the function `eval()`, which can also be used for deserialization. However, this method also interprets whatever was deserialized. This is extremely dangerous, because it opens the doors for code injection. In conclusion: If you just want to deserialize, use `JSON.parse()`.

Proprietary Key-Value Structures Some API providers manually construct their own key-value structures in JSON. JSON objects already have a native way of expressing key-value structures that should be used. If this native feature is not used, API consumers will get confused.

Treating all Properties as Mandatory API consumers sometimes treat properties as manual. By default, all defined properties are optional elements in JSON Schema. It is important to treat them that way. Optional elements allow for evolution, since old JSON objects still conform to a new JSON schema with additional properties. Optional properties are the key for developing APIs that can grow.

Assuming an Order of Properties API consumers sometimes treat properties as manual. Properties are unordered in JSON, so no assumption should be made about the order of the properties.

7.3.7.4. JSONP

JSONP stands for JSON with padding. JSONP is used by web applications, as a way to get around the same origin policy, which is enforced by web browsers. The same origin policy intends to protect the end user from malicious API calls. However, the policy even blocks non-malicious API calls.

> Recommendation: The use of JSONP is common practice and thus presented in this book. For security reasons the use of JSONP is not recommended.

JSONP provides a way to perform API calls in browsers, without getting blocked by the same origin security policy. JSONP uses the fact, that the same origin policy is not enforced on the <script> tag used in HTML. The <script> tag of HTML points to some resource containing JavaScript code, which is loaded and then executed by the JavaScript interpreter. The source of the JavaScript resource is an URL, just like any other URL. Now comes the first part of the trick: the URL of the API is provided as the source of the script.

```
<script src='https://domain.com/customers/123'/>
```

However, the browser tries to not only load the script (= call the API), it also attempts to interpret the data that was loaded. The following data is returned by the API in our example:

```
{ 'firstName': 'John', 'lastName': 'Doe' }
```

If APIs 'just' delivered data in the form of a JSON object – like APIs usually do – nothing would be done with the result of the API call. The result of the API call would be lost. Thus, the API needs to return a JSON object, which is wrapped by a call of a JavaScript function – the data is now merely the parameter of a JavaScript function.

```
process_results({ 'firstName': 'John', 'lastName': 'Doe' });
```

The JavaScript function (`process_results()` on our example) may be defined somewhere else – in the HTML page itself or in another external JavaScript, which is loaded by the `<script>` tag.

```
<script>
    process_results = function(data){
        document.write(form_name_field, data.firstName + data.lastName);
    };
</script>
```

7.4. Parameters

An API typically does not return static data. It returns dynamic data which depends on input from the API consumer, from the end user or from the client. So how can the API receive input? An API can receive input via the HTTP body and via the HTTP parameters. In the last section we have studied representations, which can be used for input via the HTTP body (see section 7.3). In this section we study the use cases for providing input via HTTP parameters (see section 7.4.1). We also describe the four HTTP parameter types (see section 7.4.2), namely path parameters, query parameters, form parameters and header parameters.

7.4.1. Use of Parameter Types

Let's start by listing different use cases for providing input to the API. The following input needs to be provided to an API:

- Resource Creation and Update (see section 7.4.1.1)
- Resource Retrieval: Filters and Sorting (see section 7.4.1.2)
- Resource Retrieval: Locators (see section 7.4.1.3)
- Resource Retrieval: Projections (see section 7.4.1.4)

- Metadata (see section 7.4.1.7)

In the following we will study each type of input and match it to appropriate parameter types.

7.4.1.1. Resource Creation and Update

When a new resource is created, the fields of that new resource need to be set with initial values. These new values need to be sent as input to the API. If a resource is created with the POST method (see section 7.5.2.2), the initial values for the fields are typically transferred as form parameters (see section 7.4.2.3). If a resource is created or updated with the PUT method (see section 7.5.2.3), the input data is sent as a representation via the HTTP body (see section 7.3). If a resource is updated with the PATCH method (see section 7.5.2.5), the input data is sent as a difference representation via the HTTP body.

7.4.1.2. Resource Retrieval: Filtering and Sorting

Collection resources (see section 7.1.3) are lists of resources. These lists tend to be long. Consumers are typically only interested in a small subset of the collection. However, transferring the complete collection to the client and performing the filtering and sorting on the client is not efficient – and in many cases – not even possible. The API needs to offer the functionality to filter collections, search in collections and sort collections.

Relational databases also offer similar functionality, so let me give you an analogy to SQL: Filtering would be realized by a WHERE clause. Sorting would be realized by the clause ORDER BY field ASC or ORDER BY field DESC.

Lets turn back to APIs and see on a couple of examples, how we use parameters for filtering and sorting. Filters are typically configured via filter criteria. Sorting requires specifying the sorting criterion and the sort order. These criteria can be regarded as modifiers on the collection resource. They are typically expressed by query parameters (see section 7.4.2.2).

Example: Filter the customers collection resource for entries with the value Mike anywhere. The value Mike could be found in the property `firstname`, in the property `lastname`, in the `address` or somewhere else.

```
/customers?search=Mike
```

Example: Filter the customers collection resource for entries with the `firstname` Mike.

```
/customers?firstname=Mike
```

Example: Sort the customers collection resource by the `lastname` property and present the results in descending order.

```
/customers?sort=lastname&sortOrder=desc
```

7.4.1.3. Resource Retrieval: Locators

Locators provide information for identifying a resource, such as a resource identifier. Let's see how the locator concept is realized in relational databases. In SQL, locators are realized in the form of a FROM clause. The value of the FROM clause may be the name of a database or the name of the table.

Relational databases are traditionally more limited in their structure than APIs. In RESTful APIs, locators are typically expressed by path parameters (see section 7.4.2.1). Path parameters in a URI path (by definition) represent a resource.

Both locators and filters may be applied to collection resources. What is the difference between locators and filters? Locators need to *identify a single element* in the collection resource. Filters do not have this stringent requirement; applying a filter on a collection may return a subset of the collection consisting of several elements.

7.4.1.4. Resource Retrieval: Projections

Sometimes, resources contain many properties or data fields. Not all consumers need the data of all these fields, and it thus makes sense to limit the resource fields to the ones needed by the consumer. This requires less bandwidth and less processing power on the side of the consumer. It thus makes sense that the API offers this functionality.

Projections select certain fields and only including those in the response. Projections provide a partial view of the resource. To be able to realize projections, JSON and XML Schema definitions need to declare most property fields as optional.

In SQL, projections are realized by the SELECT clause. For APIs, there are actually two different ways to realize projects: by query parameters and by path parameters.

Projections can be applied on both collection resources and instance resources. Let's have a closer look at a couple of examples.

7.4.1.5. Resource Retrieval: Projection on Collection Resources

If we want to select a single field from a collection resource, we use a query parameter.

Example: Return the addresses of all the customers in the customers collection resource.

```
/customers?fields=address
```

If we want to select multiple fields from a collection resource, we also use query parameters.

Example: Return only the **lastname** and the **address** of the customers collection resource.

```
/customers?fields=lastname,address
```

7.4.1.6. Resource Retrieval: Projection on Instance Resources

If we want to select a single field from an instance resource, we typically use path parameters.

Example: Return only the address of the customer with ID 123. The path parameter addresses is a projection applied to the instance resource. Note, that the path parameter 123 is a locator applied to the customers collection resource.

```
/customers/123/address
```

However, this might be considered to be a convenience function, or a shortcut. It could also be realized by query parameter.

```
/customers/123?fields=address
```

If we want to select multiple fields from an instance resource, we also use query parameters.

```
/customers/123?fields=lastName,address
```

7.4.1.7. Metadata

Each API needs authentication information and further meta data, such as information about cache management, encoding, compression or content-type. They are typically expressed in header parameters (see section 7.4.2.4). A typical example is the **Authorization** header.

7.4.2. Parameter Types

There are four different types of HTTP parameters, namely path parameters, query parameters, form parameters and header parameters. All parameters are used to provide input to the API, but in practice each type is used in a different situation. How exactly do these parameter types work? When to use which type of parameter?

7.4.2.1. Path Parameters

A URL path is used to identify a resource. A path parameters is part of the URL and thus becomes part of the resource identifier. Path parameters are thus locators (see section 7.4.1.3). Multiple path parameters are possible, but always from a tree structure. Hierarchies can be well expressed by path parameters, but lists cannot be represented.

```
https://domain.com/api/resource/{parameter-value1}/{parameter-value2}
```

If a path parameter is invalid, the URL becomes invalid, as it does not identify a resource. As a result, the resource cannot be found, and the status code `404 Not Found` is returned.

Path parameters can be used for any of the main HTTP methods GET, PUT, POST.

7.4.2.2. Query Parameters

Query parameters are key value pairs that are appended to the URL of a resource. Multiple query parameters can be concatenated, forming a list:

```
https://domain.com/api/resource?parameter1=value1&parameter2=value2
```

It is best practice to design query parameters as optional inputs for the API. Each query parameter may be provided or may be left out. If a query parameter is not present, the API should function without them or assume reasonable default values.

If a query parameter is an invalid identifier, the status code `400 Bad Request` is returned. Only if the underlying resource cannot be found, the status code `404 Not Found` is returned.

Query parameters are typically used to realize some kind of filtering (see section 7.4.1.2), but they can also be used for sorting (see section 7.4.1.2) and for projections (see sections 7.4.1.4, 7.4.1.5, 7.4.1.6). Typically they are used in combination with the GET method.

7.4.2.3. Form Parameters

Form parameters are key-value pairs, where the key is the parameter name, the value is the parameter value. Typically, they are used for data, which have been collected in a user interface with HTML forms. Form parameters are used in combination with the POST method. Form parameters are transmitted in the HTTP body. Unlike query parameters or path parameters, form parameters are not part of the URL. The advantage of using form parameters is that they are not limited by the practical URL length limitations (see section 7.2.6). The `Content-Type` of the HTTP body with form parameters is set to `application/x-www-form-urlencoded`.

In the following example a new customer resource for John Smith is created. The name of the customer is passed via form parameters. An API accepting form parameters can also be called by an HTML form.

```
POST https://domain.com/customers
firstname=John&lastname=Smith
Content-Type: application/x-www-form-encoded
-> 201 Created
```

7.4.2.4. Header Parameters

Header parameters are key-value pairs, where the key is the name of the HTTP header and the value is the parameter value. Header parameters are sent in the HTTP header, not in the HTTP body. They can be used in both requests and responses.

Typically, header parameters are used for metadata. Header parameters provide information on how to process the request or response without having to analyze the payload in the HTTP body. Header parameters are sometimes also called HTTP header fields or simply HTTP headers.

We distinguish standardized and custom HTTP headers. Most HTTP headers are standardized HTTP headers. Both clients and APIs are expected to interpret and act upon standardized HTTP header parameters. While it is possible to send custom HTTP header parameters, one cannot expect the receiver to interpret them correctly.

We also distinguish request headers and response headers: request headers (see section 7.4.2.4) are sent by clients and are interpreted by the API; response headers (see section E) are sent by the API and are interpreted by the client. Generic headers (see section 7.4.2.4) can be used in both the request and the response. See appendix D for a more complete list of header parameters.

Generic Header Parameters The header parameters describing the content, such as `Content-Length`, `Content-Language`, `Content-Encoding` and the `Content-Type`, can be used in both request and response. See appendix D for a full description. Here we explain only the most commonly used header.

`Content-Type`: specifies syntax and semantics of the HTTP body. The content-type is also called media-type or MIME-type.

Typical values of the content-type parameter are for example: `text/html`, `application/xml`, `application/json` or `text/xml`. A list of predefined content-types is maintained by IANA [24]. If possible, prefer to use registered content-types and avoid developing your own. If you need to define your own content-type and want to make it publicly available, follow IETF RFC 6838 [25].

The optional charset addition should be used whenever possible, it improves the likelihood that the data is interpreted correctly, e.g. `application/xml;charset=UTF-8`. The charset directive is provided in the content-type to avoid any encoding problems. There are default values for each content-type, e.g. the default value for `text/xml` is US-ASCII, the default value for `application/xml` is UTF-8.

If you need to define your own XML-based content-type, choose: application/vnd.domain.com.project+xml. Another example would be: application/myapp+json;v=1.

Request Header Parameters In addition to the general header parameters (see section 7.4.2.4), the following headers are commonly used in the request that is sent to the API:

- User-Agent: identifies the client (= agent). If the API is protected by OAuth or by an API key, the API can always identify the client. But if no security mechanism is used to protect the API, it is advisable that the API requires an Agent header. Why? In case many 4xx errors occur in an API, it is possible to identify if those errors originate from the same client, detect the misbehaving client and contact the responsible API consumer. Without knowing the agent or client, it is not possible to know who caused the errors; misbehaving clients are thus much harder to identify, resulting in wasted resources.

- Accept: specifies a list of media-types, which the user agent can accept as a response. This header parameter is used in content negotiation (see section 7.3.4).

- Authorization: specifies authorization credentials.

Response Header Parameters In addition to the general header parameters (see section 7.4.2.4), the following headers are commonly used in the response that is sent from the API to the clients:

- Status: HTTP status code, indicating success or the reason for failure.

- `Retry-After`: indicates how long the user agent should wait before retrying the request. Typically used in combination with 429 or 5xx status codes.

- `Location`: specifies the URL of a resource, which is relevant for this response, e.g. the URL of the recently created resource (with a `201 Created` status code) or the URL to redirect to (with a 3xx status code).

- `Allow`: lists all the methods that can be used with the respective resource. For example `Allow: GET, HEAD, PUT`

- `Server`: Just as the User-Agent identifies the software that was used to produce the request, the `Server` header identifies the software and version that was used to produce the response. It can be used to analyze interoperability problems.

7.5. Methods

If you use the REST architectural style, you need to use the HTTP protocol correctly. What does this mean? It means that you have to use all of the principles of HTTP. One such principle is the Uniform Resource Interface. It defines the basic set of operations which can be performed on any HTTP resource. If you encounter a new resource, you will feel right at home: The offered operations are all from the same set of operations offered by the uniform resource interface.

This, however does not mean that all the operations form the Uniform Resource Interface actually needs to be supported by each resource. Typically, only a subset of the HTTP methods is implemented for each resource. The provider of the API determines for each resource, which HTTP methods make sense based on business needs.

Since not all HTTP methods are supported, each resource should provide information about the implemented subset of HTTP methods. This is what the HTTP method OPTIONS can be used for.

If a client anyway attempts to interact with a resource via a method that is not supported by the resource, status code 405 Method not Allowed is returned (more about status codes in section 7.6).

7.5.1. Use of HTTP Methods

Let's look at typical operations on resources, the so called CRUD operations, which stand for creating, retrieving, updating and deleting a resource.

7.5.1.1. Retrieve a Resource

To read or retrieve information from a given resource, the GET method is used.

For example, to retrieve a listing of resources, a request with the GET method is sent to the URL of a collection resource. If the collection resource does not contain any instance resources, an empty list is returned.

```
GET https://domain.com/customers
-> 200 Ok
```

To retrieve an instance resource, a request with the GET method id sent to the URI of this instance resource. If the instance resource does not exist, a 404 Not Found status code is sent. For example:

```
GET https://domain.com/customers/1234
-> 200 Ok
{
        "firstname": "John",
        "lastname": "Smith"
}
```

The information retrieved by a GET can be cached, since GET is idempotent. Should the GET not deliver any results, it is safe to send the request again, since the GET method does not have any side-effects and is idempotent.

7.5.1.2. Create a new Resource

There are actually two ways for creating resources in HTTP.

Option 1 The first option for resource creation is to create a resource as part of a collection resource (see section 7.1.3). In this case the POST method is used and together with a collection resource a factory pattern is realized. The POST request is executed on the URL of the collection resource, to which the newly created resource is added. The initial values of the newly created resource are typically passed as form parameters (see section 7.4.2.3) in the HTTP body of the POST request. In the success case, a response is sent with status code 201 `Created` and a `Location` header containing the URI of the newly created resource.

```
POST https://domain.com/customers
Content-Type: application/x-www-form-encoded
firstname=John&lastname=Smith
-> 201 Created
Location: https://domain.com/customers/1234
```

Note, that to POST is directed towards the URL of a collection resource. A POST on the URL of an instance resource (see section 7.1.2) will return a status code 405 `Method Not Allowed`.

```
POST https://domain.com/customers/1234
-> 405 Method Not Allowed
```

And if a POST is executed on a resource which does not exists, status code 404 `Not Found` is returned.

```
POST https://domain.com/customerX
-> 404 Not Found
```

Option 2 In Option 1, a new resource was created as part of a collection resource. The resource was anonymous, since we did not need to specify its identifier or URL. The factory pattern and the POST method were used.

In Option 2, a new resource is created at a specified URL. In this case the PUT method is used. The initial values of the newly created resource are typically passed as JSON a representation or XML a representation in the HTTP body of the PUT request. The response will have status code `201 Created`. Optionally, a representation of the created resource may be returned in the HTTP body of the response.

```
PUT https://domain.com/customers/1234
{
        "firstname": "John",
        "lastname": "Smith"
}
-> 201 Created
```

If the supplied URI points to a collection resource, that status code `405 Method Not Allowed` is returned.

```
PUT https://domain.com/customers
-> 405 Method Not Allowed
```

7.5.1.3. Update a Resource

There are two options for updating a resource.

Option 1 To update the complete content of an existing resource, the PUT method is used. The complete representation is specified in the HTTP body of the PUT request.

PUT can be used for creation (see section 7.5.1.2) and for updates. The status code of a PUT request can indicate, if the resource was newly created (`201 Created`) or was updated (`200 Ok`).

```
PUT https://domain.com/customers/1234
Content-Type: application/json
{
        "firstname": "John",
```

145

```
        "lastname": "Smith-Kline"
}
-> 200 Ok
```

If the supplied URI points to a collection resource, the status code `405 Method Not Allowed` is returned.

```
PUT https://domain.com/customers
-> 405 Method Not Allowed
```

If the PUT command is performed on a resource that does not exist, the resource is created and the PUT command is interpreted as a command for the creation of the resource (see Option 2 in 7.5.1.2)

Option 2 To selectively update specific values of a resource, the PATCH method is used. It implements a partial update. It does not send the complete resource representation to the server, but only certain fields describing the difference between the new and the old version of the resource. To describe the difference between two JSON objects, two other standards can be used: JSON Patch IETF RFC 6902 [30] and JSON Merge-Patch, IETF RFC 7396 [35].

```
PATCH https://domain.com/customers/1234
Content-Type: application/merge-patch+json
{
        "firstname": "John"
}
-> 200 Ok
```

7.5.1.4. Delete a Resource

To delete a resource, the DELETE method is used. If the resource exists or has ever existed, a `200 Ok` status code is sent in the response.

```
DELETE https://domain.com/customers/1234
-> 200 OK
```

Only if the resource at the given URI has never existed, a `404 Not Found` is returned. This admittedly non-intuitive behavior ensures that the DELETE method is idempotent (see section 7.5.3.2); executing it several times yields the same result.

According to the HTTP definition, a DELETE on a collection resource would delete the entire collection. Since this is usually not desired, the DELETE is not defined on collection resources. If a client attempts to use it anyway, status code `405 Method Not Allowed` is returned.

```
DELETE https://domain.com/customers
-> 405 Method Not Allowed
```

7.5.1.5. Check Existence of a Resource

To check the existence of a resource the HEAD or the GET methods can be used. HEAD has the advantage that the cost of the call is lower than when executing a GET, since the HTTP body is not returned.

```
HEAD https://domain.com/customers/1234
-> 200 OK
```

7.5.1.6. Determine how to Call the API

Invoking the HTTP method OPTIONS on a given resource provides information on how to call the resource. Typically, no content is returned, but the HTTP header `Allow`, which lists the allowed HTTP methods.

```
OPTIONS https://domain.com/customers/1234
-> 204 No Content
Allow: GET, PUT, PATCH, DELETE
```

See section 7.9.4 for more information on how to implement discovery with the OPTIONS method.

7.5.1.7. Test the Request

To figure out how the API would receive the request, the TRACE method can be used. The API echoes back the request headers

147

it received, by wrapping them into the body of the response. The response headers are unaffected by this operation.

7.5.2. Meaning of HTTP Methods

7.5.2.1. GET

The GET method is used to retrieve information for a given resource. The GET operation is idempotent and the information retrieved by GET can be cached, and the request can be resubmitted (e.g. on a 4xx or 5xx). The GET **request** does not contain a payload, only the GET **response** contains a payload. If the resource exists, a `200 Ok` status code is returned. If the resource does not exist, a `404 Not Found` status code is returned.

7.5.2.2. POST

The POST method is typically used to create a new resource (see section 7.5.1.2). The POST method creates the new resource anonymously as part of a collection resource. The creation is anonymous, because the implementation of the POST method for the specific resource determines the URL of the newly created resource. If the client wants to determine the URL of a new resource the resource should instead be created with PUT (see section 7.5.2.3).

The POST method is also used for large queries, e.g. when a long parameter list needs to be provided. Path parameters and query parameters are limited by the maximal URL size of a specific server implementation. POST parameters are transferred as form parameters (see section 7.4.2.3) in the HTTP body and are thus not limited.

The POST method is also used for unsafe operations, for example for long running batch processes in combination with controller resources (see section 7.1.4).

Requests sent with the POST method cannot be resubmitted and cannot be cached, since they are neither safe nor idempotent.

7.5.2.3. PUT

The PUT method is typically used to modify a resource, but also for creation of a resource at a specific URL. The request typically contains a representation of the resource to be created or updated. The resource to be created or the changes to be made is expressed as a full representation in the HTTP body of the request. If a resource with the provided URI already exists, a PUT method is interpreted as a modification. If the resource does not exist, it is interpreted as a creation. The HTTP body of the request contains the new resource representation; the HTTP body of the response may be empty or may contain the new representation of the resource.

The PUT method is unsafe, but idempotent, so it can be resubmitted on a **4xx** or **5xx**.

7.5.2.4. DELETE

The DELETE method is used to delete the resource at the specified URL. The request does not contain any HTTP body. The response may contain a body, for example with the representation of the deleted resource. If the response contains a body, status code **200 OK** is returned. If the representation is not included in the body of the HTTP response, status code **204 No Content** is returned.

The DELETE method is idempotent, i.e. if it is called again in the future, it needs to provide the same response. From a practical perspective this is often not so easy to realize. If the DELETE is requested for a resource that has been deleted previously, i.e. does not exist any more, still status code **200 Ok**

149

and the representation of the deleted resource or status code
204 No Content are expected. If, however, the resource at the
given URI has never existed before and a DELETE is requested,
status code **404 Not Found** is expected. To be able to make this
distinction, the API has to keep track of all resources that have
existed at some point in time, to be able to return the right
status codes, and even needs to return the representation of the
deleted resource in some cases. To implement this practically,
either the resource is never deleted and just marked as deleted
by setting a flag.

Strictly speaking, if a DELETE method is executed on a collection resource, all resources in the collection should be deleted. Since this is often not desirable in practice, DELETE is not supported on collection resources, and a **405 Method Not Allowed** status is returned.

7.5.2.5. PATCH

The PATCH method is not part of the original HTTP standard, but it is described separately, in IETF RFC 5789 [12]. The PATCH method is used to partially update an existing resource. This means, that the client does not send the complete resource representation to the server, but only certain fields describing the difference between the new and the old version of the resource. To describe the difference between two JSON objects, two other standards can be used: JSON Patch IETF RFC 6902 [30] and JSON Merge-Patch, IETF RFC 7396 [35].

Both PATCH and PUT are used for updating a resource; what is the difference between the two? PUT is used for a complete update, and the complete resource needs to be sent to the API. Thus PUT can also be used for creating new resources. PATCH is used for a partial update, only changed fields of the resource need to be sent to the API. Thus PATCH can only be used for updating and not for creating a resource.

7.5.2.6. HEAD

The HEAD method is used for retrieving the same response that would be retrieved via GET, but without the HTTP body in the response. The HEAD method can be used for checking the existence of a resource or for reading the resource metadata. Neither the request nor the response contains any HTTP body. The method is read-only, safe and idempotent, and can thus be resubmitted.

7.5.2.7. OPTIONS

The OPTIONS method can be used for retrieving a list of the HTTP methods, which are allowed on a given resource. The request could be for example:

```
OPTIONS https://domain.com/customers/1234
-> 204 No Content
Allow: GET, PUT, PATCH, DELETE
```

The response with the `Allow` header tells the client that the HTTP methods GET, PUT and DELETE can be applied on the specified resource. Optionally, a body might be included in the response of an OPTIONS request. See section 7.9.4 for an example of using API description languages in the body of the OPTIONS response for the purpose of API discovery.

Another typical application of the OPTIONS method is in the CORS preflight as described in section 7.9.1.

An OPTIONS request is idempotent and needs to deliver the same response when resubmitted (e.g. after a 4xx or 5xx). This is rather uncritical, since an OPTIONS request is safe, i.e. read-only.

7.5.2.8. TRACE

The TRACE method is used for testing HTTP connections. When calling an API with the TRACE method, the API echoes back the HTTP headers and the HTTP body of the request. The HTTP body of the response includes the entire request including the request headers and the request body. Besides the HTTP body, the response contains its own HTTP response headers.

7.5.2.9. Non-Standard HTTP Methods

Non-standard HTTP methods should be avoided. HTTP proxies and caches need to treat these methods as unsafe and non-idempotent. Non-standard HTTP methods have been used e.g. in the WebDAV Project. Examples are: MOVE, LOCK, UNLOCK, PROPATCH, PROPFIND.

> Recommendation: Instead of inventing non-standard HTTP methods, use the POST method.

7.5.3. Properties of HTTP Methods

HTTP methods have two important properties: HTTP methods can be safe and idempotent [16]. Knowing the implications of these properties is especially useful for the API clients.

Why is it relevant to distinguish safe and unsafe HTTP methods? Safe methods can be used by spiders or by web caches for pre-fetching without altering the state of the resource.

Why is it relevant to distinguish idempotent and non-idempotent methods? Clients might send a request, wait for the answer, but do not receive a response. If the method is idempotent, the client can simply resend the request. If the method is non-idempotent (e.g. initiating a bank transfer), the client would need to check if the previous request was executed and roll it back, before attempting a retry. Without the check, two banks transfers may be initiated.

7.5.3.1. Safe

In general, safe methods do not have side effects, do not change the state of the resource and are read-only. Note, that the value of the resource can still change, e.g. caused by a backend change or by another methods. GET, HEAD and OPTIONS are safe HTTP methods. POST and PUT are unsafe.

7.5.3.2. Idempotent

In general, idempotent methods can be repeated without altering the end result. Executing the method multiple times has the same effect as executing the method only once. It functions similar to a setter method in programming. This is relevant in the failure case, e.g. when a method does not return. Then the idempotent property ensures that the method can be executed again. In short: Idempotent actions are repeatable without unexpected side-effects.

It is clear, that all safe methods (GET, HEAD and OPTIONS) are idempotent. PUT is also idempotent because it completely replaces the state of an existing resource with the payload passed in the request. POST is non-idempotent since it appends the payload passed in the request to an existing resource collection. Each time the POST is executed, the resource is growing in length.

Thus we have the following list of idempotent HTTP methods: GET, HEAD, OPTIONS, PUT, DELETE. All major HTTP methods are idempotent, except for POST.

7.6. Status Codes

The use of HTTP status codes is an important principle of HTTP and of REST. So what is a status code and what is it used for? When a method is executed on the HTTP resource, it returns at least a status code as response. It basically indicates the success or failure of the operation. But there is much more detailed information associated with a status code. This allows the client to use the status code to determine the next steps after calling the API. For example:

- If a temporary problem exists on the server, it could retry later.

- If the request was malformed, the client could rewrite the request and resend the corrected request.

- If the requested resource was moved, the request could be performed on the new address of the resource.

For each of these common success and error cases, the HTTP status code is defined as a numerical code and a short human readable description. For example, the numerical status code (e.g. 200) is supplemented with a short one- or two-word description (OK). When mentioning specific status codes in this book, we always use the numerical code and the short description together (200 OK) to improve the readability of the text.

The set of status codes and their meaning is standardized in IETF RFC 7231 [14] and IETF RFC 6585 [28]. In the following sections, we study the meaning of the most common status codes. In Appendix E you can find a full list of status codes and their meaning.

7.6.1. Overview of HTTP Status Codes

The numerical status code consists of 3 digits, for example 201. The first digit groups the status codes into five groups:

- Informational (1xx) status codes: Non-critical information.

- Success (**2xx**) status codes: The request was processed successfully.

- Redirection (**3xx**) status codes: The client has to do another request based on the header parameters received in the response.

- Client Error (**4xx**) status codes: An error occurred. The client is responsible for the problem.

- Server Error (**5xx**) status codes: An error occurred. The server or API is responsible for the problem.

The informational and success codes are relatively easy to handle. More consideration has to be given to the status codes indicating redirection and error. They are explained in the following sections.

7.6.2. Redirection

If you move to a new house and change your address, your mail might still arrive at your old address. This is annoying, so you typically have your mail redirected to your new address. A similar scenario occurs when APIs are moved to a new address. Clients will still call the old URL when trying to reach the API. So requests – just like the mail in the above example – need to be redirected.

Redirection could be realized on the server-side or on the client-side. For the server-side solution, we would install a proxy on the server, which forwards the requests to the new address. The server-side solution would be transparent to the client. For the client-side solution, we merely send a message back to the client, saying "we moved, you can reach us under this new address".

HTTP offers a client-side redirect solution. It standardizes the message sent back to the client with the new address. HTTP status codes **3xx** are used to indicate a redirect to another address and the new address is transmitted via HTTP header, in the location header variable.

There are several status codes for redirection, each with a slightly different meaning. The last digit provides some meta information about the new address:

- **301 Moved Permanently**: Redirect permanently to the address in the `Location` header.

- **302 Moved Temporarily**: Redirect temporarily to the address in the `Location` header.

- **303 See Other**: Redirect to the address in the `Location` header, changing the HTTP method to GET.

- **307 Temporary Redirect**: Redirect to the address in the `Location` header, preserving the original HTTP method.

Note, that the server does not retrieve the content from the new address, the client need to to this. The server - in this case the API - merely indicates the new address to the client via `Location` header.

7.6.3. Error Handling

For the interaction in a distributed system, it is essential that both parties (client and API) agree, how to behave if an error occurs. To achieve this common agreement, conventions such as status codes are very valuable for error handling. The standardized HTTP error codes describe, which party (client or API) is responsible for fixing the error: There are errors that should be fixed by the client (see section 7.6.3.1) and errors that need to be fixed by the server (see section 7.6.3.2).

7.6.3.1. Client Errors

Client errors are indicated by a **4xx** status code. These errors can be fixed by the client. The API should not leave the client alone with the status code, but should provide a good error message (see also section 7.6.3.3), which enables the client to fix the error. The error message should state how to get more information, provide documentation about the error and describe how the error can be fixed. It is best practice to include a link to a publicly accessible documentation of the error on a web page.

Incoming requests to the API should be validated (see also section 7.7), including parameters and payload in the HTTP body. The following client errors indicate a malformed request.

- **400 Bad Request**: The request is syntactically incorrect. For example: the request contains query parameters that cannot be processed.

- **404 Not Found**: The requested resource is not found, e.g. a non-existing resource-id was specified as path parameter.

- **405 Method Not Allowed**: The HTTP method specified in the request is not allowed. The API needs to return a list of supported HTTP methods in the **Allow** header.

- **406 Not Acceptable**: The API cannot produce a response in any of the media-types that the client can accept.

- **415 Unsupported Media Type**: If the API expects input in the HTTP payload, the **Content-Type** header of the request needs to be set to the appropriate media-type of the input. If the API cannot process data of the supplied media-type, it returns a **415 Unsupported Media Type** status code.

- **422 Unprocessable Entity**: The input is in the appropriate content-type, is syntactically correct, but is semantically wrong (i.e. it does not make sense to execute).

- **429 Too Many Requests**: The user send too many requests per time window.

The following authentication and authorization status codes are typically used. Often status codes 403 and 401 are confused.

- **401 Unauthorized**: The request failed because the user is not authenticated in the first place. Credentials are missing or are incorrect.

- **402 Insufficient Funds**: This may be triggered by monetized APIs. The request failed because the authenticated user does not have a sufficient funds, or a sufficiently large API plan.

- **403 Forbidden**: The request failed for an authenticated user, who does not have authorization to access the requested resource.

7.6.3.2. Server Errors

Server errors cannot be fixed by the client or by the end user, the API or server is responsible for fixing this type of errors. A 5xx status code is used to indicate an error in the API or server.

It is best practice to inform the clients, when the server error will be fixed and when the client can retry to send the request. This can be done by including the HTTP header field `Retry-After` with the delay in seconds in the response. Here an example, which suggests that the error is fixed in one hour (3600 seconds).

```
GET https://domain.com/customers/1234
-> 500 Internal Server Error
Retry-After: 3600
```

```
{
  "id": "database",
  "message": "The database is currently unavailable.",
  "description": "We restore data after a hardware failure.
      No data was lost. Retry later.",
  "url": "https://domain.com/docs/redundant-data-storage"
}
```

For server errors, good logging is essential to be able to find the root cause of the problem. The problem is likely a bug in the implementation of the API or an error in the backend system. In addition to logging, an alert to operations or even the developer should be sent for critical errors, e.g. via a support forum or dedicated Slack channel.

- `500 Internal Server Error`: Some unexpected condition occurred in the API, e.g. an exception was thrown.

- `501 Not Implemented`: The functionality requested by the client is not implemented yet.

- `503 Service Unavailable`: The server cannot fulfill the request or may refuse the connection.

7.6.3.3. Error Message

The API can use HTTP status codes for communicating errors to the client. However, the information contained in the status code alone is not sufficient. In addition to the HTTP status code, an error message should be returned in the HTTP body of the response.

When the HTTP status code is not enough to describe the error, and a structured machine-readable error message should be provided, it is best practice to structure the error message according to IETF RFC 7807 [33].

But even if you don't want to go so far as to use this IETF standard for the error messages of your API, at least the structure of the error message should be consistent across all APIs in the API portfolio, or across all APIs of an API provider. A good start is to define a consistent error code structure for this message, for example a JSON structure. Use it across your API portfolio. It should contain: A brief message describing the error in a few words, a longer description including instruction on how to fix the error, an identifier of the error so this error can be found in the code, and optionally a link to more information.

Example for status code 402 `Insufficient Funds`

```
GET https://domain.com/customers/1234
-> 402 Insufficient Funds
Retry-After: 60
{
  "id": "rate_limit",
  "message": "Account reached its API rate limit.",
  "description": "You have purchased our Silver Plan
                              with up to 3000 requests/min.
                              Purchase our Gold Plan.",
  "url": "https://domain.com/docs/rate-limits"
}
```

If an HTTP status code representing an error is returned, provide a link to the documentation or API description, which specifies error handling and how to call the API correctly.

7.7. Input and Output Validation

Input validation (see section 7.7.1) ensures that the input in HTTP request body and HTTP parameters is correct and complete. It is essential for an API.

Output validation (see section 7.7.2) ensures that the output created by the API and sent via the HTTP response body is correct and complete. It is optional for an API, depending on the integrity level one tries to achieve for the API.

7.7.1. Input Validation

Incoming requests to the API should always be validated, including parameters and payload in the HTTP body. The goal of input validation is an improved developer experience. Thus, input validation should be as gentle, graceful and forgiving as possible. How can gentle, graceful and forgiving input validation be realized?

There should be no required parameters or at least as few required parameters as possible. As many parameters as possible should be optional. A sensible default value should be defined for the optional parameters to guarantee a predictable default behavior.

If additional, unrecognized query parameters are sent, the API should just ignore them. The API should never fail due to unexpected query parameters it receives, as long as the request is syntactically correct. If required parameters are missing, an error with status code 4xx needs to be thrown.

Send the following 4xx status codes for failed input validation:

- **400 Bad Request**: The request is syntactically incorrect. One could validate by checking the syntax of the query parameters, header parameters and the syntax of the HTTP payload. If the HTTP payload is a JSON object, one may check that it actually conforms to a predefined JSON schema. Similarly, an XML object should be checked for conformance to an XML Schema.

- **404 Not Found**: The requested resource is not found.

- **405 Method Not Allowed**: The HTTP method specified in the request is not allowed.

- **406 Not Acceptable**: The API cannot produce a response in any of the media-types that the client can accept.

- **415 Unsupported Media Type**: The API cannot process the media-type that was used for serializing the HTTP body in the request.

- **422 Unprocessable Entity**: The input is semantically incorrect.

7.7.2. Output Validation

Optionally, the response produced by the API can be validated before it is sent to the client. If clients expect a high integrity of the API, the output should be validated. In any other case the output is typically not validated, as validation costs compute cycles, which adds to the latency of the API. For example, consumers might expect a higher integrity level from APIs in the financial sector than from APIs in the entertainment sector. Due to the high importance of integrity, additional latency is acceptable for these APIs.

To implement output validation, one could check if the representation conforms to the serialization rules. JSON representation need to conform to a predefined JSON schema, XML representation need to conform to a predefined XML schema. If the schema validation fails, send a `500 Server Error` status code and flag it in the server log as an urgent issue. It is likely a bug.

7.8. Intuitive Use

It is important that consumers can use the API intuitively. But what does *intuitive use* mean in this context? It means that the API consumer does not need to look up every detail in the documentation when using the API. Rather, the API consumer should be able to guess URIs, parameter names and data fields. Now, the question is: How can we design our APIs for *intuitive use*?

If the API is really intuitive, only the API consumers can tell. But with our API design we should fulfill the preconditions for intuitive use. One precondition for enabling intuitive use is *consistency*. We should use guidelines, conventions and standards as much as possible to achieve consistency.

To some extent we already use a convention to achieve consistency by subscribing to the REST architectural style. The architectural style provides some constraints and guidelines regarding the architecture and interaction scheme, but the REST constraints still leave a lot of room for individual design, for example regarding the names of headers, fields, parameters and URLs. To create even better preconditions for intuitive use, we need to introduce additional guidelines that ensure harmonization and consistency for the names used in the API.

7.8.1. Consistent Names and Naming Schemes

To support *intuitive use* within one API and across the complete API portfolio, the names should ideally be consistent. For example: The same name `user-id` might be used as a data field in a root resource, as a URI fragment in a nested resource, and as a query parameter. All three occurrences of the name should have at least consistent spelling.

A naming scheme could be used to provide guidelines and consistency. In the following we have a list of competing naming schemes (see section 7.8.1.1) and a list of different elements that have a name. We then discuss which naming schemes typically apply for each named element.

7.8.1.1. Typical Naming Schemes

In the following, typical schemes for names are presented. The naming scheme is applied to the name of the naming scheme itself, thus the following list is not only a list of naming schemes, but also a list of examples.

- camelCase: JSON fields/properties typically follow camelCase, since this is the standard notation for JavaScript

- lowercase: Query parameters and path parameters are typically formatted in lowercase.

163

- Header-Case: There is a list of standardized header parameters in the HTTP RFC. These standardized HTTP parameters are formatted using the Header-Case. It is recommended to format additional, non-standardized header parameters in Header-Case. There are typically no intersections between names of header parameters and other names.

- snake_case: PHP developers typically use this naming scheme.

- PascalCase: Java developers typically use this naming scheme for their classes.

7.8.2. Summary

It is best practice to establish a naming conventions, which are consistently used all throughout the API portfolio. An additional challenge for the consistent naming is, that APIs connect different technological worlds and each of these worlds has established its own naming conventions. When connecting these worlds by means of APIs, one of these competing conventions has to be explicitly selected, to achieve overall consistency.

See these listing of naming schemes as an inspiration for specifying naming schemes for your own APIs or API portfolio. There is no right or wrong naming scheme. The important thing is that a naming scheme is specified, and that consistent names are chosen with this naming scheme.

7.9. Integration

It should be easy to integrate the API. This has implications on the frontend design. It should be possible to call the API with JavaScript in the browser (see section 7.9.1), it should be possible to explore the API via the browser address bar (see section 7.9.2) and the API should be robust to incorrect user input (see section 7.9.3).

7.9.1. Cross-Origin Resource Sharing (CORS)

It should be possible to call the API with JavaScript in the browser. Modern browsers, however, prevent this for security reasons, unless it is explicitly allowed via a mechanism called Cross-Origin Resource Sharing (CORS) [37].

To protect end-user from malicious scripts, browsers implement a security policy – the same origin policy. The policy prevents websites from making client-side AJAX (Asynchronous JavaScript and XML) calls to APIs, which come from a different origin than the website. What exactly counts as "same origin"? For two resources to have the same origin, their URLs have to have the same scheme (protocol), same host and same port. Subdomains are considered to be different hosts. The intent of the same origin policy is the prevention of cross-site scripting (XSS) and cross-site request forgery (CSRF).

However, it also affects legal API calls made through JavaScript in the browser. If a consumer wants to integrate an API via JavaScript on her website, the browser would apply the same origin policy and prevent the API call. What can the API provider do, to make sure the API works, even if called by third party websites? The API can actually configure the browser's security to allow the call. The API does this by sending an HTTP header which lists all website URLs, which may legally call the API.

The process for configuration works as follows: Before the actual API request is sent, the browser sends a so called pre-flight request to the API. The purpose of the pre-flight request is the collection of the `Access-Control-Allow-Origin` header, which contains the security configuration. Depending on the security configurations received in response to the pre-flight request, the browser allows the subsequent API call.

1. The browser performs the pre-flight request. It uses the OPTIONS method, even though the real API request may use another HTTP method, e.g. a GET. The browser sends the pre-flight request to the URL of the intended API call. The intended API call is described in the `Origin` request headers and metadata about the intended API call, such as custom content-type, custom HTTP headers and the HTTP methods it intends to use.

2. The API needs to process the pre-flight request. It needs to implement the OPTIONS method, read the `Origin` request header and send the `Access-Control-Allow-Origin` header in response if it determines that the API call is legitimate based on the provided data. The value of this header is a list of URLs, which are allowed to perform cross-origin requests. A list of origins can be used, or a wildcard (*) allowing access from any origin.

3. The browser checks the `Access-Control-Allow-Origin` headers. If they match the intended API call, the browser send the API call request.

7.9.2. Browser Exploration

APIs are designed for consumption by machines (apps), and machines will not use the browser to consume the API. However, developers might explore APIs when considering whether to consume this API or the API of a competitor. Usability and browser exploration is an important criterion from a marketing and developer-experience perspective. This is why APIs should be explorable and discoverable in the browser if possible.

If this is desired, there are implications for versioning (see section 11.5), formatting of responses (see section 7.3), pretty printing of responses (see section 11.2.5), limit the use of headers - replicate lots of header information into the representations in the HTTP body (see section 7.4.2.4).

7.9.3. Robustness

Robust APIs can take a lot of "abuse" from clients. They are also forgiving when confronted with unspecified or wrong user input (see section 7.7.1). Often, consumers do not know the right parameter values, so designing the API for intuitive use is helpful (see section 7.8). In addition, a robust API can be called without parameters, by internally using default parameter values. These need to be documented, to achieve a predictable behavior.

7.9.4. Discovery

Invoking the HTTP method OPTIONS on a given resource provides information on how to call the resource. The OPTIONS method should be supported by all resources. There is a basic OPTIONS implementation, which strictly supports what the HTTP standard defines. And there is an advanced OPTIONS implementation, which provides additional meta information that s relevant for calling APIs.

In a basic implementation the response is status code `204 No Content` with the HTTP header field `Allow`, containing a comma separated list of HTTP methods, which are used with this resource.

```
OPTIONS https://domain.com/v1/books
-> 204 No Content
Allow: GET, PUT
```

A more advanced implementation of the OPTIONS method delivers an API description, e.g. in RAML or Swagger. By specifying the desired format in the `Accept` header, the API may deliver different representations of the API description, e.g.

WADL, RAML (see section 9), Swagger (see section 8) and a HTML documentation.

```
OPTIONS https://domain.com/v1/books
Accept: application/swagger+yaml
-> 200 OK
swagger: '2.0'
info:
  title: Book API
  description: The book API
  version: v1
host: domain.com
schemes:
  - https
basePath: /v1
produces:
  - application/json
paths:
  /books:
    get:
      summary: Book listings
      description: Provides a list of all
                   available books written
                   in a specific language
...
```

8. OpenAPI/Swagger for API Frontend Design

When designing a new API, you need to make a lot of API frontend design decisions. You should capture these design decisions using an API description language (see chapter 4). Such an API description language is Swagger. The Swagger specification is maintained by the OpenAPI group, so the language is sometimes also called OpenAPI. RAML is an alternative and it is introduced in the next chapter. You really only need to have an API description in one of the two languages. In this chapter we will learn how Swagger can be used to capture the previously introduced API frontend design decisions (see chapter 7).

8.1. Introduction

This description is based on Swagger v2.0. It is not a replacement for a complete and thorough introduction to Swagger. This section intends to provide some intuition for the usage of Swagger.

There are actually two variants of Swagger 2.0, one variant has a JSON syntax and the other variant has a YAML syntax. Only the YAML syntax is presented here. The basic syntax of YAML applies, which uses whitespace for structuring. A YAML file is hierarchically structured and consists of properties, which are realized as key-value pairs and objects. Objects have child properties, which are indented with whitespace. It is possible to have lists as values, they are presented in squared brackets

169

[]. There can also be lists of properties, in this case a minus - is used in front of each property in the list.

An API description in Swagger contains the following main information items:

Basic information and meta-information, such as name, title, and location of the API and user documentation. This information is captured in the root element. A list of resources including methods, schemas and parameters Reusable elements such as data definitions, responses, parameters and securityDefinitions Example

Let's get started by looking at the API portfolio of an online book store. This API portfolio contains two APIs, one collection API delivering a listing of all the books and a book API, providing details for a specific book, which is identified by an ISBN. In the following we describe this API portfolio using Swagger.

```
swagger: '2.0'
info:
  title: Book API
  description: The book API ...
  version: v1
host: domain.com
schemes:
  - https
basePath: /v1
produces:
  - application/json
paths:
  /books:
    get:
      summary: Book listings
      description: Provides a list of all
                   available books written
                   in a specific language
      parameters:
        - $ref: '#/parameters/languageSelection'
      responses:
        200:
          description: A listing of the books
          schema:
            type: array
            items:
              $ref: '#/definitions/Book'
  /books/{isbn}:
    get:
      summary: Book information
      description: Information about the
                   book with the specified
                   ISBN
      parameters:
        - name: isbn
          in: path
```

```
              description: ISBN of the book to get
              required: true
              type: string
          responses:
            200:
              description: The book with the
                           given ISBN
              schema:
                $ref: '#/definitions/Book'
          security:
            - oauthImplicit: [read_books]
  parameters:
    languageSelection:
      name: lang
      in: query
      description: select the language
                   of the books
      type: string
  definitions:
    Book:
      properties:
        title:
          type: string
        author:
          type: string
        price:
          type: string
        isbn:
          type: string
        language:
          type: string
        description:
          type: string
      example:
        title: Walden,
        author: Henry David Thoreau,
        price: 8.90,
        isbn: 123456789X,
        language: en,
        description: A reflection on simple
                     living in nature
  securityDefinitions:
    basicAuth:
      type: basic
    apiKeyAuth:
      type: apiKey
      name: api_key
      in: header
    oauthImplicit:
      type: oauth2
      authorizationUrl: https://domain.com/oauth/auth
      flow: implicit
      scopes:
        write_books: modify books
        read_books: read books
```

As you can see in the example, Swagger is a hierarchically structured language. Sub elements are indented relative to their parent elements.

All elements of this example are taken apart and explained in

171

the following subsections.

8.2. Root Element

The root element is at the top of the Swagger description. It is used to describe basic information about the API and to provide some meta information. The root element includes the following properties:

- `host`: The property host specifies the host name or IP address of the host, on which a running instance of the API or an API simulation are or will be deployed.

- `basePath`: The basePath is the part of the URI of the API, which follows directly after the host name. It points to a running instance of the API or of an API simulation.

- `schemes`: The schemes in the root element are the default protocols used for this API. The scheme property can have the values `ws`, `wss`, `http`, `https`. It can be overwritten per method.

- `consumes`: The consumes property defines the media-types consumed by the APIs.

- `produces`: The produces property defines the media-types produced by the APIs.

- `info`: The property info specifies meta information about all the APIs in the portfolio. It includes fields such as

    - `title`: Title of the API portfolio.
    - `description`: Description of the API portfolio.
    - `termsOfService`: Link to a terms of service description for the API portfolio.

- `contact`: Contact information, including name, email, URI.
- `license`: Link to the license of the API portfolio.
- `version`: Version of the API portfolio.
- `paths`: The path property defines the resources of the API. We will study this element closer in the section on resources.

- `responses`: Reusable definitions of responses. We will study this element closer in the section on resources.

- `parameters`: Reusable definitions of parameters. We will study this element closer in the section on parameters and in the section on reusable elements.

- `definitions`: Reusable definitions of data structures. We will study this element closer in the section on reusable elements.

- `securityDefinitions`: Reusable definitions of security schemes. We will study this element closer in the section on security.

- `security`: Default security for this API, references one of the securityDefinitions. We will study this element closer in the section on security.

8.3. Resources

Resources are described in the paths property. Each resource is identified by its relative path (relative to the `basePath`). For each resource, a number of HTTP methods (GET, POST, PUT, DELETE, etc.) can be listed. For each method, the following properties can be defined:

173

- **summary**: One line summary describing the purpose of the resource.

- **description**: Verbose description of the resource.

- **schemes**: The schemes of this particular method. The scheme property can have the values `ws`, `wss`, `http`, `https`.

- **security**: The security mechanism, which is used to protect this API.

- **parameters**: List of input parameters, which can be provided for this API. Different types of input parameters (query parameter, header parameter, form parameter or path parameter) are supported. These parameter types are described in more detail later in this chapter.

- **responses**: List of response types, which can be expected from this API. The response types are identified by their status code. Responses are described in more detail later in this chapter.

- **consumes**: The media-types consumed by the resource.

- **produces**: The media-types produced by the resource.

- **operationId**: Unique name of this resource.

An example of a resource with a GET method:

```
swagger: '2.0'
paths:
  /books:
    get:
      summary: Book listings
      description: The book listings
                   based on a title
      schemes: https
      security:
        oauthImplicit
          - read_books
      parameters:
        ...
      responses:
        ...
      produces: application/json
```

Each method of a resource offers a list of possible responses. Responses are identified by the HTTP status code they provide. A response has the following properties:

- `description`: Description of the response.

- `schema`: Definition of the HTTP body of the response. It can be a primitive type (string, number, integer, boolean, file), an array or an object.

- `headers`: Header parameters of the response. It is structured in a similar way as the header parameters of the request.

- `examples`: An example response.

```
swagger: '2.0'
paths:
  /books/{isbn}:
    get:
      summary: Book listings
      responses:
        200:
          description: Successful response
                       with a book listing
          schema:
            $ref: '#/definitions/Book'
          examples:
            application/json:
              title: Walden
              author: Henry David Thoreau
              price: 8.90
              description: A reflection on simple
                           living in nature
              isbn: 123456789X
```

8.4. Schema

Swagger differentiates schema definitions and schema references. Schema references merely refer to a previously defined schema. Schema definitions are used to define a data structure. They are properties of the root element. They are based on the abstract syntax of JSON Schema [10]. If Swagger is used in the YAML

175

variant, the schema definition can be expressed in the concrete syntax of YAML, as shown in the following snippet.

Besides the specification of the data structure, a schema definition may also include an example instance of the data structure.

```
swagger: '2.0'
definitions:
  Book:
    properties:
      title:
        type: string
      author:
        type: string
      price:
        type: string
      isbn:
        type: string
      language:
        type: string
      description:
        type: string
    example:
      title: Walden,
      author: Henry David Thoreau,
      price: 8.90,
      isbn: 123456789X,
      language: en,
      description: A reflection on simple
                   living in nature
  ErrorModel:
    type: object
    required:
      - message
      - code
    properties:
      message:
        type: string
      code:
        type: integer
        minimum: 100
        maximum: 600
  ExtendedErrorModel:
    allOf:
      - $ref: '#/definitions/ErrorModel'
      - type: object
        required:
          - rootCause
        properties:
          rootCause:
            type: string
```

The data definitions can describe JSON or XML data structures depending on the MIME-type declared in the surrounding element of the schema reference. For XML data structures, additional information about the mapping from the Swagger data definition to XML schema can be provided in the `xml` property. It contains child properties such as `name replacement`, declaration of the `namespace`, or declaration of the `prefix`. The keyword `attribute` indicates if a property should be translated into an attribute or an element.

8.5. Parameters

Several types of parameters are supported. All parameters have the following properties:

- `name`: Name of the parameter

- `type`: Data type of the parameter. It can be string, number, integer, boolean, file, array

- `in`: Type of the parameter. Values can be `path`, `query`, `formData`, `header`, or `body`. Interestingly, the HTTP body is listed as an input parameter.

- `schema`: Schema of the HTTP body of the request. It is only available if the property `in` is set to `body`. The schema is usually not defined in place, but it is referenced, e.g.
  ```
  $ref: '#/definitions/User'
  ```

- `required`: Indicates if the parameter is optional or required. Can be true or false.

- `description`: A verbose description of the parameter.

- `format`: Additional formatting rules for the parameter values.

- `items`: Describes the elements in an array. It is only available if type is set to array.

- `collectionFormat`: Format for serializing an array. Possible values are: `csv`, `ssv`, `tsv`, `pipes`, or `multi`. The default value is `csv`.

```
swagger: '2.0'
paths:
  /books/{isbn}:
    get:
      summary: Book information
      parameters:
        - name: isbn
          in: path
          description: ISBN of the
                       book to get
          required: true
          type: string
      responses:
        ...
```

Path parameters are described by `in:path`. For path parameters a placeholder is defined in the path of the resource. The name of the placeholder is the name of the parameter.

Query parameters are described by `in:query`. Form parameters are described by `in:form`. Header parameters are described by `in:header`. Input parameters, which are provided in the HTTP body, are described by `in:body`.

8.6. Reusable Elements

When describing a complete API portfolio containing several APIs, API descriptions would be quite repetitive. This is actually a good sign, since it shows that API governance was applied on the API portfolio to ensure consistency. Elements which are consistently applied throughout the description of the API portfolio, can be factored out into reusable elements.

Some elements of a Swagger description can be reused by declaring them once in the root element and referencing them later. The reusable elements can be parameters, schemas and responses. References to reusable elements are realized by the reference object. It has the following format.

```
$ref: '#/definitions/Book'
```

Reusable parameters can be declared in the **parameters** property of the root element.

```
swagger: '2.0'
parameters:
  skipParam:
    name: skip
    in: query
    description: number of items to skip
    required: true
    type: integer
    format: int32
```

Reusable schemas can be declared in the **definitions** property of the root element.

```
swagger: '2.0'
definitions:
  Book:
    properties:
      isbn:
        type: string
      title:
        type: string
```

Reusable responses can be declared in the **responses** property of the root element.

```
swagger: '2.0'
responses:
  NotFound:
    description: Entity not found.
  IllegalInput:
    description: Illegal input for operation.
```

8.7. Security

Swagger differentiates the abstract definition of the security schemes and the binding of the security schemes to a particular API.

8.7.1. Security Definition

A list of security schemes is abstractly defined in the property **securityDefinitions**. Each item in the list has a name and

179

the following properties:

- `type`: Type of the security scheme. Possible values are `basic`, `apiKey` or `oauth2`.

- `description`: Description of the security scheme.

- `name`: Name of the header or query parameter, which contains the apiKey. Only relevant for `type:apiKey`.

- `in`: Indicates if the `apiKey` is transmitted as header or query parameter. Can have the values `query` or `header`. Only relevant for `type:apiKey`.

- `flow`: Indicates the OAuth grant type and can have the values `implicit` (for implicit grant), `password` (for resource owner password credential grant), `application` (for client credential grant) or `accessCode` (for authorization code grant). Only relevant for `type:oauth2`.

- `authorizationUrl`: URI of the OAuth authorization endpoint. Only relevant for `type:oauth2`.

- `tokenUrl`: URI of the OAuth token endpoint. Only relevant for `type:oauth2`.

- `scopes`: Available OAuth scopes. Maps the name of the scope to a short description of the scope's meaning. Only relevant for `type:oauth2`.

An example for a security definition.

```
swagger: '2.0'
securityDefinitions:
  basicAuth:
    type: basic
  apiKeyAuth:
    type: apiKey
    name: api_key
    in: header
  oauthImplicit:
    type: oauth2
    authorizationUrl: https://domain.com/oauth/auth
```

```
          flow: implicit
        scopes:
          write_books: modify book listings
          read_books: read book listings
```

8.7.2. Security Binding

Each operation can use its own security scheme, by referencing one of the declared security definitions. For OAuth security schemes, a list of the required scopes is provided.

Example for API keys:

```
swagger: '2.0'
paths:
  /books:
    get:
      summary: Book listings
      security:
        apiKeyAuth: []
```

Example for OAuth:

```
swagger: '2.0'
paths:
  /books/{isbn}:
    get:
      summary: Book information
      security:
        oauthImplicit:
          - read_books
```

181

9. RAML for API Frontend Design

When designing a new API, you need to make a lot of API frontend design decisions. You should capture these design decisions using an API description language (see chapter 4). Such an API description language is RAML, it is an alternative to Swagger introduced in the previous chapter. You really only need to have an API description in one of the two languages. In this chapter we will learn how RAML can be used to capture the previously introduced API frontend design decisions (see chapter 7).

9.1. Introduction

RAML is an API description language, which was invented by Mulesoft. Spelled out, RAML stands for the RESTful API Modeling Language. In addition to the language, a set of RAML tools are offered for describing, producing, consuming, and visualizing RESTful APIs. RAML is supported by some API platforms, such as Mulesoft Anypoint, 3scale and Restlet.

This description of RAML is based on RAML v0.8. It is not a replacement for a complete and thorough introduction to RAML. This section intends to provide some initial ideas for the use of RAML. The language specification is available on `http://raml.org/spec.html`.

RAML is based on YAML. YAML describes hierarchical data structures - similar to XML, but uses whitespace for structuring.

Compared to XML, YAML is more lightweight and more readable. A YAML file consists of properties, which are realized as key-value pairs, objects or lists. Keys are strings and values can be primitive types or lists. Lists are presented in squared brackets [], e.g. `securedBy: [oauth_1_0, oauth_2_0]`. There can also be lists of properties, in this case a minus - is used in front of the property. Objects have child properties, which are indented by whitespace.

An API description in RAML contains the following main information items:

Basic information and meta information about the API, such as name, title, location and user documentation. This information is captured in the root element. Resources including methods, schemas and parameters. Reusable elements including resource types, traits and security declarations. Example

Let's get started by describing the Book API portfolio in RAML. It is the same API portfolio we have used in the previous section for the description in Swagger. This API portfolio contains two APIs, one collection API delivering a listing of all available books written in a given language, and a book API providing details for a specific book, which is identified by an ISBN. In the following we describe this API portfolio in RAML.

```
#%RAML 0.8
title: Book API
baseUri: https://domain.com/{version}
version: v1
mediaType: application/json
protocols: [https]
documentation:
  - title: Start page for the
          documentation of the API
    content: |
      The book API ...
resourceTypes:
  - collection:
      get:
        description: returning a list
                     of elements, which
                     are part of the
                     collection
      post:
        description: adding a new element
                     to the collection
traits:
```

```
    - languageSelection:
        queryParameters:
          lang:
            type: string
/books:
  type: collection
  get:
    is: [ languageSelection ]
  /{isbn}:
    uriParameters:
      isbn:
        type: string
    get:
      responses:
        200:
          body:
            application/json:
              schema: |
                { "$schema": "http://json-schema.org/schema",
                  "type": "object",
                  "description": "A book",
                  "properties": {
                    "title":   { "type": "string" },
                    "author":  { "type": "string" },
                    "price":   { "type": "number" },
                    "isbn":    { "type": "string" },
                    "language":    { "type": "string" },
                    "description": { "type": "string" }
                  },
                  "required": [ "title", "author", "isbn" ]
                }
              example: |
                { "title": "Walden",
                  "author": "Henry David Thoreau",
                  "price": 8.90,
                  "isbn": "123456789X",
                  "language": "en",
                  "description": "A reflection on simple
                                  living in nature"
                }
```

All language elements you can find in the above example are explained in the following subsections.

9.2. Root Element

As you can see from the example, RAML is a hierarchical language. Sub elements are indented relative to their parent element. The parent element of them all is the root element at the top of the RAML description. It is used to specify some basic information. It includes the following properties:

- `title`: The title is a human readable name of the API.

- `baseUri`: The baseUri points to a running instance of the API or of an API simulation. The version can be part of the baseUri and can be referenced as a URI template parameter.

- `version`: The version of the API.

- `mediaType`: The mediaType specified in the root element is the default media-type for this API portfolio. It can be overwritten per method.

- `protocols`: The protocols in the root element are the default protocols. It can be overwritten per method.

- `schemas`: Schemas define data structures, typically in the form of JSON Schemas or XML Schemas. They can be specified inline or can be included from an external file.

- `documentation`: User documentation is provided in the form of a title and some descriptive text.

- `securitySchemes`: Predefined security packages.

- `traits`: Reusable parts for a method definition.

- `resourceTypes`: Reusable parts for a resource definition.

Resources

Resources are direct child elements of the root and are identified by their relative URI. The resource URI must begin with a slash (/). Resources can be nested, where nesting is expressed by indenting the relative URI.

For each resource it is defined, which HTTP methods may be executed. All basic HTTP methods are supported, such as GET, POST, PUT and DELETE. Multiple HTTP methods can be used for each URI.

```
#%RAML 0.8
title: Book API
/books:
  get:
    responses: !include get.raml
  post:
    responses: !include post.raml
```

For each HTTP method multiple responses can be specified. The responses are identified using HTTP response codes. Each response consists of a specification for header and body.

```
#%RAML 0.8
title: Book API
/books:
  get:
    responses:
      200:
        body: !include body.raml
        header: !include header.raml
      400:
        description: Invalid Request
      500:
        description: Internal Server Error
```

The body is specified by providing the content-type, a schema definition and an additional example. Multiple representations of the same resource can be served on the same URI, same method and same response code. The representations are differentiated only by the content-type.

```
#%RAML 0.8
title: Book API
/books:
  get:
    responses:
      200:
        body:
          application/json:
            schema: !include book.json
            example: |
              { "title": "Walden",
                "author": "Henry David Thoreau",
                "price": 8.90,
                "isbn": "123456789X",
                "description": "A reflection on
                                simple living
                                in nature"
              }
```

9.3. Schema

The schema definition is expressed as JSON Schema [10]. The schema can be declared inline or it can be included from an external source.

```
#%RAML 0.8
title: Book API
/books/{isbn}:
  uriParameters:
    isbn:
      type: string
  get:
    responses:
      200:
        body:
          application/json:
            schema: |
              { "$schema": "http://json-schema.org/schema",
                "type": "object",
                "description": "A book",
                "properties": {
                   "title":   { "type": "string" },
                   "author":  { "type": "string" },
                   "price":   { "type": "number" },
                   "isbn":    { "type": "string" },
                   "description": { "type": "string" }
                },
                "required": [ "title", "author", "isbn" ]
              }
```

9.4. Parameters

In RAML, path parameters are declared as properties of the resource and all other types of parameters are declared as properties of the method. All named parameters have the following properties:

- displayName: A human readable name.

- description: Documentation of the parameter.

- type: Data type of the parameter. The data type can be string, number, integer, data, boolean, file.

- enum: For parameters of type string, enum allows to define a list of all valid string values.

- `pattern`: A regular expression (ECMA 262/Perl 5) that values must satisfy.
- `minLength`: Minimum number of characters in a string value.
- `maxLength`: Maximum number of characters in a string value.
- `minimum`: Minimum integer value.
- `maximum`: Maximum integer value.
- `example`: Example value for this parameter.
- `repeat`: Indicates how many times the parameter can occur.
- `required`: Indicates if the parameter must be present (true/false).
- `default`: default value for this parameter.

9.4.1. Path Parameters

Path parameters are called `uriParameters` in RAML. They are declared on two locations. The location of the value of the path parameter is marked by the parameter name in curly braces `{}` within the relative URI path. To provide additional information about the parameters, it is also listed under the `uriParameters` element. This allows for the declaration of the parameter type and any of the other parameter properties listed above.

The books API can be called by `GET /books/123` for example.

```
#%RAML 0.8
title: Book API
/books/{isbn}
  uriParameters:
    isbn:
      type: string
```

9.4.2. Query Parameters

Query parameters can be declared for each HTTP method separately. The books API can be called by `GET /books?isbn=123` for example.

```
#%RAML 0.8
title: Book API
/books:
  get:
    queryParameters:
      isbn:
        type: string
```

9.4.3. Form Parameters

Form parameters can be declared for each HTTP method separately. The books API can be called by `POST /books`. The body contains the data `isbn=123`.

```
#%RAML 0.8
title: Book API
/books:
  post:
    formParameters:
      isbn:
        type: string
```

9.4.4. Header Parameters

Header parameters can be declared for each HTTP method separately. The books API can be called by `GET /books`. The HTTP header contains for example the entry `isbn: 123`.

```
#%RAML 0.8
title: Book API
/books:
  get:
    headers:
      isbn:
        type: string
```

9.5. Reusable Elements

The description of a consistent API portfolio can be quite repetitive. Repeatedly used elements should be factored out and thus become reusable elements. Reusable elements are declared once and referenced several times. In RAML, there are two categories of reusable elements. External reusable elements can be included from separate files and internal reusable elements can be referenced from the same RAML file.

9.5.1. External Elements: Inclusion of Files

RAML offers the possibility to include the content of an external file. The referenced file is inlined by a pre-processor. Including an external file is a form of reuse.

External reusable elements can be the right hand side of any YAML declaration, i.e. anything right of the colon. In the following example, the property with name `external` retrieves its value from an included text file.

```
external: !include myTextFile.txt
```

9.5.2. Internal Elements: Definition of Resource Types and Traits

Internal reuse, i.e. reuse within the same RAML file, can be achieved by `resourceTypes` and `traits`. `resourceTypes` are partial resource definitions and are applied on resource definitions. A `trait` is a partial method definition and is applied on methods.

Both `resourceTypes` and `traits` are defined in the root element of the RAML document. In the following section we show how the `resourceTypes` and `traits` can be used in API specifications.

```
#%RAML 0.8
title: Book API
version: v1
resourceTypes:
  - myCollection:
      get:
        description: returning a list of
                     elements, which are
                     part of the collection
      post:
        description: adding a new element
                     to the collection
        is: [ languageSelection ]
traits:
  - languageSelection:
      queryParameters:
        lang:
          type: string
```

As a side note: A `trait` can even be used for defining one of the `resourceTypes`. This is shown in the above example. The trait `languageSelection` is used within the definition of the resourceType `myCollection`.

9.5.3. Internal Elements: Usage of Resource Types and Traits

`resourceTypes` are applied by the keyword `type` as a direct child of the resource. `traits` are applied on method level or on resource level by the keyword `is` followed by a list of the applied traits. If the `trait` is applied on resource level, it applies to all methods of this resource.

```
#%RAML 0.8
title: Book API
/books:
  type: collection
  get:
    is: [ languageSelection ]
```

9.6. Security

RAML language constructs for security describe how the API is protected. This is usually a two-step approach. First, one or several `securitySchemes` are configured.

Then these `securitySchemes` are bound to an API, to a resource or to a specific HTTP method of a resource via the keyword `securedBy`. By using this two-step approach, it is easy to achieve a consistent application of the same `securitySchemes` on several resources and APIs.

A `securityScheme` is basically a configuration, which specifies the type of the security mechanism (OAuth 1.0, OAuth 2.0, Basic, Digest, or a wildcard for another mechanism), the available OAuth grant types, available OAuth scopes, parameters, headers, responses and URIs of the different OAuth endpoints. The `securitySchemes` need to be declared as part of the root element. Security schemes, e.g. for OAuth, can be defined inline or – more often – in separate files.

```
#%RAML 0.8
title: Book API
securitySchemes:
    - oauth_2_0:
        description: |
            OAuth 2.0 security mechanism.
        type: OAuth 2.0
        describedBy:
            headers:
                Authorization:
                    description: |
                        Send the OAuth 2 access
                        token as Bearer token
                        in the Authorization Header
                    type: string
            responses:
                400:
                    description: |
                        Invalid request.
                401:
                    description: |
                        Bad or expired token.
                403:
                    description: |
                        Bad OAuth request.
        settings:
            authorizationUri: https://domain.com/oauth2/auth
            accessTokenUri: https://domain.com/oauth2/token
            authorizationGrants: [ code, token ]
            scopes: [administrator, user]
```

In a second step, the defined `securitySchemes` can be bound to APIs, resources or methods. There are two ways to do this: either as default security, or as security for a specific API, resource or method.

Default security is applied to all resources of the API. This can be achieved by the keyword `securedBy` on the root element. The default can be overwritten by specifying the `securedBy` keyword on the respective API, resource or method.

When applying securitySchemes with the `securedBy` keyword, a list of allowed `securitySchemes` can be specified. If this list contains more than one element, the listed `securitySchemes` are alternatives.

```
#%RAML 0.8
title: API
version: v3
baseUri: https://domain.com
securitySchemes:
 - oauth_2_0: !include oauth_2_0.raml
securedBy: [ oauth_2_0 ]
/admin:
  get:
    securedBy: [ oauth_2_0: {
                  scopes:[administrator],
                  authorizationGrants:[code]
                }
              ]
```

For each `securityScheme`, additional parameters can be specified, such as the OAuth scopes and OAuth grant types, which are required for this particular element. The scopes and grant types, which are listed under `securedBy` should be a subset of the available scopes and grant types that were declared in the `securitySchemes`.

10. API Backend Design Decisions

There are two approaches for building APIs, the green field approach and the legacy approach. API frontend design and architectural design is the same for both approaches, but these approaches differ mainly in the way they realize backend design and where they place the business logic.

- Green field approach: This approach is typically used by startups, which do not need to take care of legacy systems. With the green field approach the API provider may implement the business logic directly as part of the API. RESTful services are constructed from scratch to realize the business logic. These are exposed as APIs, either directly or via an API platform.

- Legacy approach: This approach is typically used by large enterprises with a big IT landscape. APIs are exposed via an API platform. The API uses existing backend services, which provide the business logic and business data. An API may connect to one or even multiple backend systems. These backend systems are typically legacy systems and are not very user-friendly.

In this chapter we study the legacy approach. For the legacy approach it is relevant to design the backend connections, transformations and aggregations.

10.1. Backends

For large enterprises, the business logic and business data typically reside in backend systems. These backend systems are legacy systems whose interfaces are relatively complex, not very intuitive, not very user-friendly and non-standard.

APIs present the data from the backend systems in a bite-sized, clean, clear, consumer-friendly and approachable manner. APIs change the outward appearance of the already existing business logic. Under the surface, the APIs call the legacy backends to access data or business functionality.

Backends typically provide the data for the API, but they come in all shapes and forms: They may use a proprietary protocol, use proprietary data formats or present the data in an unsuitable structure. It is the task of the API to mediate between the clean RESTful frontend of the API and the "ugly" legacy backend. The data provided by backends typically needs to be transformed, before it can be exposed by an API.

An API may connect to one or multiple such backend systems, in which case the data needs to be combined, enriched, transformed and filtered. The API orchestrates the calls to different backend systems, secures and protects the data and services and ensures the performance and availability of the complete system.

To connect to backends, connection details are needed, such as credentials and URIs. These connection details are ideally not hard coded into the API, but they are configured, originating from a configuration management system. This makes it easy to connect to the respective systems in the different environments (development, test, pre-production, production).

10.2. Transformations

Transformations modify a source object and create a target object as outcome. The source object can be the request that the API has received from its client, the target is then a request to the backend system. The source object can also be the response from the backend system, the target is the API response that is sent out as a response to the client.

Incoming requests and incoming response are the two possible sources of the transformation, outgoing request and outgoing response are the two possible targets of the transformation (see section 10.2.3).

Several transformation tasks need to be performed (see section 10.2.2), such as transforming data structure, transforming representations and mediating security.

We have different transformation tools at our disposal (see section 10.2.3), and choose the appropriate tool depending on where the source information is found (HTTP body or parameters), the content type (usually JSON or XML) of source target.

10.2.1. Transformation Source and Target

First, the request that the API has received from its client needs to be transformed into a request to the backend system. We call it request transformation (see section 10.2.1.1). Then the response from the backend system needs to be transformed to an API response that can be sent out to the client. We call it response transformation (see section 10.2.1.2).

10.2.1.1. Request Transformation

Each incoming RESTful API request has to be transformed into an outgoing request to the backend. This request needs to conform to the protocol of the backend. To call the backend services, request objects need to be prepared, which are subsequently sent to the backend system. Transformations can create the request objects based on information that was received in the API request, received from another backend call or is already present as static information.

10.2.1.2. Response Transformation

In a similar manner, the response from the backend needs to be transformed into a RESTful response of the API. To obtain relevant data from backend services, the responses received from backend systems need to be transformed and relevant data needs to be extracted. The data received from the backend systems is likely not in the right format and needs to be transformed again, this time into a response object.

10.2.2. Transformation Tasks

Whereas APIs typically apply the RESTful architectural style, backends may use a wider variety of protocols, such as RPC (remote procedure calls), SOAP or message queues. The task of the API is to translate between the different protocols. What you typically need to transform:

- Transforming data structure (see section 10.2.2.1)
- Transforming representations (see section 10.2.2.2)
- Mediating security (see section 10.2.2.4)

10.2.2.1. Data Structure Transformation

Often, the structure of the data needs to be adapted. The API typically has a simple data structure, focusing on a specific use case, whereas the backend system might require a more complex data structure. For example, the API might offer a flat list of shopping cart items, whereas the backend requires a deeply nested data structure to represent the shopping cart.

To transform the data structure, you can use transformation languages or the data extraction and template mechanism (see section 10.2.3).

10.2.2.2. Representation Transformation

A representation transformation is used if you want to preserve the structure of the data and just change the way the data is represented. An example is the transformation from JSON to XML or from XML to JSON. Changing the representation is quite simple, especially because you can find existing libraries for the major programming languages to convert between representations. There are, however, a couple of things to take care of, as described in the next section.

10.2.2.3. Conversion between JSON and XML

Conversions between JSON and XML typically need to be performed in enterprise scenarios, since JSON is offered towards consumers and XML is provided by backend systems.

It is best practice to preserve the structural integrity of the resource when converting between XML and JSON. Structural integrity is desirable during transformations, as it ensures support for round trip transformations. It also means that no information needs to be added and no information is lost during transformations.

Differences between JSON and XML XML data needs to be structured as a tree with a named root element. JSON does not require a hierarchical root element and if there is a root element in JSON, it does not need have a name. Thus the transformation from JSON to XML will need to create a named root element - even if there is none in JSON.

What is an Envelope Object? An envelope object is a slight modification of a JSON object. The envelope object introduces named root elements to lists of properties if they do not already exist.

We start with the following JSON object (without a named root element):

```
{
  "id" : 123,
  "name" : "Joe"
}
```

We generate the corresponding envelope object:

```
{
  "customer" : {
    "id" : 123,
    "name" : "Joe"
  }
}
```

Envelope objects are used for conversion from JSON to XML, since XML always requires a named root element.

Round Trip Conversion: JSON to XML and back to JSON In a round trip conversion, we first transform from JSON to XML and then from XML back to JSON. If the conversion preserves structural integrity, the JSON data before and after the round trip should be the same. However, when an envelop object is introduced during the transformation from XML to JSON, the envelope object has to be converted back to JSON. This artificially introduced envelope object cannot be distinguished from original data, and it will become part of the JSON object. The conversion introduced data. As a result, the JSON data we started with is different from the data after the round trip conversion.

Practical Tips for the Conversion Ideally, a predefined method is used for the conversion between XML and JSON. There are a lot of intricate details that one can get wrong, for example in the encoding.

JSON should not be created by XSL. When extracting values with XSL (depending on you XSL implementation) they can contain characters, which are invalid in Javascript, such as quotes or line breaks.

If you need to program the conversion, I recommend to first construct a JavaScript object and then serialize the object using `JSON.stringify()`. This method does all the required encoding.

10.2.2.4. Security Mediation

Backends are internal systems that are not directly accessible from the internet. For protection, they have their own set of security mechanisms. To access backends, technical user accounts are typically required. The API needs to provide the credentials, such as those of a technical user, for accessing the backend systems. In addition you might propagate the identity of the end user, e.g using SAML or JWT. Often, however, the end user identity is just included in the payload of the backend request.

10.2.3. Transformation Tools

The tool box for transformations needs to contain parsers for JSON, XML and URL objects. It should be possible to extract single values from the objects and to construct entire objects from single values.

Transformation Languages To transform XML data you can use XSLT [38]. JSON does not provide a dedicated Transformation language, so typically the data extraction and template mechanism is used.

Data Extraction and Template Mechanism With this mechanism, you write a template of the target (e.g. a backend request or an API response). The template looks like a real backend request, but contains placeholders, which are replaced by data extracted from the API request. Typically, the placeholders are replaced by values from the HTTP body or from the parameters (HTTP header parameters, path parameters or query parameters) of the API request.

How to extract data from the HTTP body? Complex data structures are typically in the body of the HTTP request and are formatted as a JSON object. You can use [19] to extract data from JSON objects or JSON Pointer IETF RFC 6901 [31], which is considerably less powerful. To extract data from XML objects, you can use XPath [9].

10.3. Dealing with Backend Errors

Backends may fail and throw an error. As caller of the backend, the API needs to deal with these errors. It can either attempt to fix the error or communicate the error to the API client. Errors of the backend system should not be routed directly to the client but need to be interpreted, translated and improved according to the frontend design (see section 7.6.3 on error handling), before sending the error to the client.

Status codes from the backend should not be simply forwarded to the client, as illustrated on a couple of examples: If the backend sends a 2xx status code, the API might still fail, e.g. because of an unsatisfied output validation of the API. If the backend sends a 5xx status code, the error might be caused by the client (then the API should return a 4xx) or it might be caused by the API (then the API should return a 5xx). If the backend sends a

4xx status code, the API or the client of the API has caused the error. The status code and even the error messages may need to be analyzed and translated. Depending on the root cause of the error, this means that the API should deal with the error in one of the following ways:

- Attempt to fix the request to the backend right away and re-send the request to the backend.

- Fail with a 4xx status code to the client if the error is caused by an input of the client.

- Fail with a 5xx status code to the client if the root cause of the error is in the API or in the backend.

Analyzing the root cause is not always easy, even if the backend uses correct HTTP status codes. But this is not always the case with legacy backend systems: the backends may not use the correct status codes to communicate the errors, or may not provide a proper error message. I have seen many backend systems that always return a 200 status code, even in the error case. Instead of forwarding the incorrect status codes, the API needs to fix this behavior, so proper status codes (see section 7.6) and error messages (see section 7.6.3.3) are returned.

The error messages from the backends may need to be masked for security reasons. As a general guideline for implementing APIs, implementation details should be hidden – and for errors, this is especially true. Avoid the exposure of stack traces or other internal errors, e.g. those coming from backends. Avoid to leak names or versions of the technology being used. The reasons for hiding details error messages:

- Clients might break when changing the details of the error message.

- Lock-in is created for a specific technology.

203

- Security concerns are raised, since this information could help potential attackers of the system.

10.4. Logging

It is important to perform adequate logging for APIs. Without proper logging it is a challenge to hunt for bugs and to ensure traceability. A logging system, such as Splunk, is required to manage the log data, especially with high traffic. A balance between too little and too much logging has to be found to achieve an adequate level of verbosity.

10.4.1. Sanitizing Logged Data

APIs deal with personal data, deal with credentials and perform authentication. Sensitive information, such as personal data, access tokens, authorization codes or other credentials should not be logged and the logs need to be anonymized.

10.4.2. Require a Transaction ID / Request ID / Tracking ID

Request IDs are unique IDs, generated by the client for each request. The same request ID is passed on to each system in the call stack of the API, and thus to all the backend systems. Request IDs help to track the request even in busy log files, where many requests arrive within a short time window. The path of the request from the API to the backend systems can so be tracked and errors can be identified.

Require that the caller supplies a unique request ID in the HTTP header sent to the API. The response should also contain this request ID. If backends systems are called by the API, pass this request ID along to the backend.

11. Non-Functional Properties of APIs

To be usable in practice, APIs should not only be functionally correct, but they need to expose favorable non-functional properties, such as security, performance and evolvability.

APIs need to be secure (see section 11.1). We introduce security concerns that need to be addressed and both mechanisms and best practices for ensuring security in our APIs.

APIs also need to have a high performance and high availability (see section 11.2). We introduce several techniques for improving API performance: e.g. pagination, caching (see section 11.3), traffic shaping (see section 11.4).

APIs needs to be evolvable: It has to be easy to update the feature set of the API and roll out new versions of the API without breaking existing clients (see section 11.5).

11.1. Security

APIs provide a selective and controlled access to the assets of the enterprise. These new possibilities for access come with the responsibility for ensuring the security of the enterprise assets. Security is thus a critical concern for APIs.

11.1.1. The Appropriate Level of Security

As APIs provide new windows into the enterprise for making business with your consumers, these new windows can also be used by hackers to get into the systems of the enterprise. Exposing the systems via APIs thus creates a range of new security challenges. In this section we analyze the variables that determine an appropriate level of security.

There is a trade-off between security and usability of a system. Highly secure systems might introduce many hassles for the user up to the point where the systems become practicably unusable. However, systems that are just designed from a usability perspective, often do not address important security concerns, leaving the system at risk for destabilization, service outages or theft of private data. A balance between security and usability is needed.

Security cannot be a one-size-fits-all solution that is uniformly applied to all APIs. Instead, each API needs to be analyzed separately and appropriate security mechanisms have to be identified for each API.

The first step is determining the need for protection or the security level of a particular API. Such an analysis needs to take place during the design phase of the API. The security level actually needs to be analyzed according to several dimensions, we call them security concerns (see section 11.1.2). For each security concern the criticality and sensitivity of the exposed data and the vulnerability of the connected backend systems is analyzed.

Based on the outcome of the analysis, appropriate security mechanisms (see section 11.1.3) are chosen to protect the API in a second step. It is important that the security mechanism is appropriate for the particular API. If the chosen security mechanism is too strict, the usability of the API suffers and consumers might look for alternatives to this API. If the security mechanism is too weak, there is a higher risk for private customer data or business data to get stolen, or for IT systems to get destabilized.

11.1.2. Security Concerns

Each API needs to be analyzed for its needs for protection along the following security concerns.

11.1.2.1. Authentication

Authentication determines if a user is really who she claims to be. Usually both clients and end users need to be authenticated by API providers. Authentication may have different strengths, depending on the authentication mechanism and the authentication processes.

11.1.2.2. Authorization

Authorization determines which APIs and data an authenticated user is allowed to access. For example, an authorization rule might state that customers are only allowed to use the profile API, whereas trusted partners are allowed to use the complete API portfolio. Another authorization rule might limit the data which is returned by the API, for example the users should only see data about their own account and not data about others accounts.

11.1.2.3. Delegation

An app would like to access an API to get some data that only the end user is authorized to access. In this scenario, the user needs to delegate her access rights to the app. This could be accomplished if the end user provides her credentials to the third party app. However, this simple delegation pattern is not secure. With the end user's credentials, the third party app has full access to the end user's account. The access cannot be limited to certain data or to certain operations. Instead, a secure delegation method needs to be used.

11.1.2.4. Identity

An app would like to obtain profile information about the end user, such as the end user's name, address, birthday and nationality. This information contains private information and needs to be especially protected. The end user needs to consent to the use of her identity attributes.

11.1.2.5. Attacks

APIs are publicly exposed and sooner or later they will face attacks. Typical attacks include SQL injection, XML document structure attacks, certificate attacks, or denial of service attacks. The API itself or an appropriate security component need to put mechanisms in place to prevent these attacks.

11.1.2.6. Integrity of API Input and Output

If the input and output of the API is critical, the integrity of the data needs to be ensured. There are two cases: (1) Data should not be read by anyone except for the specified receiver. (2) It should be ensured that the data originates from the specified sender it should be noticed if the information has been modified by a third party.

11.1.3. Security Mechanisms

In this section we introduce security mechanisms for APIs and mention how they address the security concerns introduced previously.

11.1.3.1. API Keys

An API key is a unique identifier, which is required for calling the API. The API key identifies a specific API consumer and a specific set of APIs which the API consumer is authorized to call. The API key can thus be used for both authentication and authorization. The API consumer is supposed to keep the API key confidential.

The API key is generated and managed by the API engagement platform and by the API runtime platform. On the API engagement platform, the API consumer can request an API key for a specific API or set of APIs. The API engagement platform is typically run as a self-service portal.

When calling the API, the client provides the API key as a parameter in the request. The API runtime platform verifies the provided API key against the database of API keys, and thus authenticates the API consumer. The runtime platform also authorizes the request by verifying that the called API is in the set of APIs, which are allowed to be called with this key. Now the runtime platform can perform logging, analytics and monetization charges on the account of the respective API consumer.

API keys provide a lightweight mechanisms for authentication (11.1.2.1) and authorization (11.1.2.2) of the API consumer. The end user cannot be authenticated with the API key mechanism, but only the API consumer. API keys are vulnerable to capture and replay attacks, thus one needs to make sure the API key cannot be captured. API keys should only be used in combination with TLS (see section 11.1.3.7).

11.1.3.2. HTTP Basic

HTTP basic is a simple mechanism for authentication and authorization of an API request. It is standardized in IETF RFC 7235 [13], and it is widely used, since it is supported by many HTTP libraries and servers. The API consumer first requests the API credentials on the API engagement platform, and uses them when performing the API call, providing username and password in the `Authorization` header of HTTP. HTTP basic can also be used with a challenge-response mechanism:

1. The client requests the protected resource

2. The server sends a `401 Unauthorized`, along with the HTTP header `WWW-Authenticate: Basic`

3. The client adds credentials to the request by filling the `Authorization` header and sends the request again.

Typically, the credentials are sent directly, starting with step 3. Step 3 requires the following header field:

```
Authorization: Basic base64encode({username}:{password})
```

Where `base64encode()` is a function for encoding the argument in base64. Note, that base64 encoding can be easily reversed and does not provide any protection for the cleartext password. The password is sent in cleartext and thus needs to be protected by TLS (see section 11.1.3.7). HTTP basic primarily addresses the security concern of authentication (11.1.2.1), but also authorization (11.1.2.2).

11.1.3.3. HTTP Digest

HTTP digest follows the same principles as HTTP basic, but it is a bit more secure. It is standardized in IETF RFC 7235 [13]. It uses a challenge-response mechanism, consisting of the following steps:

1. The client requests the protected resource

2. The server sends a `401 Unauthorized`, along with a Header field `WWW-Authenticate: Digest realm="{realm-value}", nonce="{nonce-value}"`

3. The client adds credentials to the `Authorization` header of the request

All three steps are necessary, since the client requires the nonce-value which is provided by the server. In step 3 the following header field is required:

```
Authorization: Digest username="{username}", realm="{realm-value}",
nonce="{nonce-value}", uri="", cnonce="{cnonce-value}",
nc="{nc-value}", qop="{auth-method}", response="{response-value}"
```

The response-value is calculated as follows:

```
response-value=md5hash(md5hash({username}:{realm-value}:{password}):
{nonce-value}:{nc-value}:{cnonce-value}:{auth-method}:
md5hash({http-method}:{uri}:md5hash({http-body-value})))
```

Where:

- `username` and `password` are provided by the app.

- `realm-value` and `nonce-value` are provided by the API server in step 2.

- `uri` is the URI of the protected resource or API.

- `cnonce-value` is the nonce of the client. It is randomly generated and only to be used once. It is used to present replay attacks.

- `nonce-value` is the nonce of the server. It is randomly generated and only to be used once. It is used to present replay attacks.

- `nc-value` is a request counter.

- `http-method` is the HTTP method, such as `GET`, `POST`, `PUT`, `DELETE`.

- `http-body-value` is the HTTP body.

- `auth-method` is the quality of protection provided by the authentication method. Possible values are `auth` or `auth-int`.

HTTP digest primarily addresses the security concern of authentication (11.1.2.1), but also authorization (11.1.2.2).

11.1.3.4. OAuth

In previous sections we have studied the security mechanisms API keys, HTTP Basic and HTTP Digest. They can be used when two parties are involved: the API consumer and the API provider. The API consumer needs to provide a secret (= password) as part of the API request, and the API provider authenticates and authorizes the request.In API scenarios, typically a third identity is involved, the identity of the end user. This allows scenarios, where a third party app of an API consumer gets access to the personal data of the end user via API. It might sound complicated, but it is a very common pattern in API design.

An example: Tim wants his tweets from Twitter to appear automatically on LinkedIn, so he can stay in touch with his business contacts. To realize this functionality, LinkedIn would need to have access to Tim's Twitter account, to read the tweets. In this example, Tim is the end user, the third party app and API consumer is LinkedIn, and Twitter is the API provider.

OAuth is a standard for delegating authorization, it is standardized in IETF RFC 6749 [22]. With OAuth, Tim gets an access token from Twitter and provides it to LinkedIn, thereby delegating his access rights to LinkedIn. The token represents the access rights for a subset of the data, for a short time frame. LinkedIn uses the access token to call the APIs of Twitter.

An example for an OAuth protected API call:

```
GET https://domain.com/myAccount
Authorization: Bearer wG88jZ6xyp4
-> 200 OK
{...}
```

OAuth offers four grant types, which are used in different scenarios and can replace API keys, HTTP Basic and HTTP Digest. OAuth is the most popular and most secure way to protect an API. The exact interactions for the different OAuth grants should be studied by any API designer. Check out this book [3] on API Security with OAuth.

The OAuth standard primarily addresses the security concern of delegation (11.1.2.3), but complete OAuth solutions also address authentication (11.1.2.1) and authorization (11.1.2.2).

> OAuth is the recommended mechanisms for delegation, authentication and authorization for APIs.

11.1.3.5. OpenID Connect and JWT

OpenID Connect is a standardized identity layer on top of OAuth. It is specified by the OpenID Group[34]. By design, OAuth does not expose the identity of the end user towards the API consumer. Only an access token is provided to the API consumer, which is nothing more than an identifier - a random string - to the API consumer. The access rights are not encoded into the access token, but only associated to this identifier.

OpenID Connect extends OAuth by an additional token, the ID token, and by an additional API, the userinfo API. The userinfo API is protected by OAuth and provides additional identity information about the user. The ID token holds identity information, such as first name, last name and email address. This information is actually contained in the ID token, and the token contains a cryptographic signature of the OpenID Connect server.

The ID token is formatted according to JSON Web Token standard (JWT), defined in IETF RFC 7519 [6]. JWT can be used to represent and transfer claims in a secure manner. Claims are represented as JSON data structures. The claims object can be signed according to JSON Web Signature (JWS) [5] to ensure integrity or encrypted according to JSON Web Encryption (JWE) [23] to ensure privacy.

> OpenID Connect primarily addresses the security concern of identity (11.1.2.4) and is the recommended choice in the context of APIs. JWT is used by OpenID Connect and ensures the integrity of the information (11.1.2.6).

11.1.3.6. Access Restrictions by IP, Location and Time

Access to the API can be limited to a certain IP address range. Using such a security mechanism, one can for example limit access to clients from the enterprise internal network.

It is possible to limit API-based access to a certain time of the day or a certain day of the week. The security of some APIs may be improved by limiting access only to business hours.

On mobile phones and tablets, but even on more and more notebooks, location information is available. This may be retrieved from a GPS sensor or though 3G or Wifi network triangulation. With this location information, it is possible to limit the API access to a certain geographic area. The mechanism is called geo-fencing.

IP-, location- and time-restrictions primarily address the security concern of attacks (11.1.2.4).

11.1.3.7. X.509 Transport Layer Security (TLS)

Don't do APIs without TLS. The security of API keys, HTTP Basic Authentication and OAuth 2.0 depends on TLS, and thus the security of most API calls. Just reject requests without TLS by dropping requests or by sending an HTTP status code `403 Forbidden`. TLS ensures the confidentiality and integrity of information in the HTTP body, header and in the URI; TLS thus protects the integrity of input and output of the API.

Two-way TLS protection is a strong type of transport security, since it allows to identify the API consumer. However it is not suited for the mass market, instead it is mainly used for the secure point-to-point integration with trusted partners.

TLS/SSL implementations are increasingly under attack. The list of TLS/SSL vulnerabilities is growing, with the heartbleed and shellshock attacks, POODLE (Padding Oracle On Downgraded Legacy Encryption) and FREAK (Factoring Related Attack on RSA Keys).

TLS is the basis for many of the security mechanisms used for APIs. Thus, always upgrade your security infrastructure and API platform to support the latests TLS versions.

11.1.3.8. Visibility Levels

Not all APIs are publicly visible. The access to some APIs is restricted via network configurations to the internal network or to the partner network. This restriction is usually distinct from authorization, but visibility is a precondition for authorization.

Typical visibility levels are:

- Public: APIs can be offered publicly, so they can be reached by anyone. Authentication and authorization may limit the access further.

- Private/Internal: APIs can be offered privately, so they can only be reached from inside the enterprise. If you really need private APIs, protect them by client certificates.

- Partner: APIs can be offered to partner only, so they can be used by a selected list of partners only. Authentication and authorization may limit the access further.

11.1.3.9. Validation

Conservative input and output validation is a valuable security mechanism to prevent attacks (see 11.1.2.5). See also section 7.7 on input and output validation.

Input validation is used to protect the API from unintended input. Unintended input can for example be discovered by schema validation on the HTTP body of the request. Certain types of attacks, such as SQL injection, or code injection can be discovered by specialized pattern matching algorithms.

Output validation can be used to avoid leakage of the data. Schema validation can be used to enforce that all objects sent out have a specific format – nothing else is allowed.

Validation should be applied on all input and output parameters, such as header-, query-, path- and form-parameters and on the HTTP body. Schema validation on unstructured values – usually part of parameters – is implemented using regular expressions. Schema validation on the HTTP body is implemented using JSON Schema for JSON and XML Schema for XML objects.

11.1.3.10. Threat Protection

The security infrastructure should protect against SQL injection attacks and code injection attacks. Often, heuristic pattern detection methods are used for this purpose. In addition, all APIs should be developed defensively and according to best coding practices to avoid common security issues.

11.1.3.11. Traffic Shaping

Traffic shaping (see section 11.4) mechanisms such as rate limitation, spike limitation or quotas can be used for protecting against denial of service attacks.

11.1.4. Security Best Practice

Knowing that nothing can be a 100% secure, you should at least rely on best practices in security. These best practices provide a baseline, an commonly accepted agreement of a reasonable level of security.

11.1.4.1. Ensuring Confidentiality and Integrity of Information in URIs

Using TLS protects the confidentiality and integrity of information. It should always be applied for API traffic. For an additional level of protection, sign or encrypt sensitive data.

To detect URI tampering, create a signature of the sensitive part of the URI and transfer it as an additional query parameter. The value of this query parameter should be base64-encoded and URL-encoded. To ensure that the request originated from a certain sender, a signature can be used as well. If the data should stay confidential and can only be shared with a selected few, encryption should be used. To protect confidentiality of the URI parameters, encrypt the sensitive part of the URI and transfer it as a query parameter. The value of this query parameter should be base64-encoded and URL-encoded.

An alternative approach for securing the input to APIs is the use of JSON Web Tokens (see section 11.1.3.5). The input parameters can be encoded in the JWT and the JWT is either signed or encrypted. The token is transferred and the receiver may inspect the signature to verify the integrity of the data.

11.1.4.2. Treat All APIs as Public APIs

Some APIs may intentionally just never be publicly advertised, so no one can find them. Such APIs are typically integrated into in-house apps and are intended to be used exclusively by the in-house apps.

This might create a false sense of security, and relying only on the secrecy of the URL as the only security mechanism. But the app can be decompiled and the URI to the API can be retrieved. Not advertising an API and relying on it as the only security measure is risky.

At least an additional security mechanism for authentication and authorization needs to be added. It would be even better to make the APIs public. A public API can still protected, e.g. by OAuth. In addition once may use a very strict policy for on-boarding new API consumers.

11.1.4.3. Known Vulnerabilities and Known Attack Patterns

Security components or libraries should be used to provide mechanisms for preventing known attacks. The attack patterns need to be continuously updated. Implementing the attack pattern recognition in the API itself is not recommended.

11.1.4.4. Protect All APIs with OAuth by Default

OAuth offers four grant types, which are used in different scenarios and can replace API keys, HTTP Basic and HTTP Digest. OAuth is the most popular and most secure way to protect an API. The exact interactions for the different OAuth grants should be studied by any API designer [3].

11.1.4.5. CORS

CORS is used to allow other sites to call the API from the browser. It selectively switches off a security feature of the browser. Thus, one needs to be very restrictive when using CORS. For more details on CORS, see section 7.9.1.

11.2. Performance and Availability

End users are generally extremely sensitive to waiting time and have little patience for long API response times. If API requests cannot be handled quickly, end users will not use the app, so the app builder and API consumer will eventually choose an alternative API. Performance is an important non-functional property for the user-acceptance of the API. In this section we propose mechanisms to improve the performance of the API.

11.2.1. Caching

By storing frequently used data, caching can increase the performance of the API significantly. In the distributed system consisting of client app, API and backend, caching can be performed both by the client and by the API. We identify these common use cases in section 11.3.1. In section 11.3.2 we introduce the mechanisms for implementing caching and focus on the HTTP caching mechanism 11.3.3.

11.2.2. Traffic Shaping

When an API gains in popularity, for example, because a marketing campaigns for the API goes viral or the app of one or several consumers gains in popularity, the traffic on the API platform will increase sharply. Increasing demand for APIs is certainly desirable from the perspective of the API provider. However, if the increased demand is sudden and unexpected, it might lead to high latency, a degradation of the response time, low throughput and even to unavailability of the API.

A mechanisms for ensuring a certain performance and availability is traffic shaping. See section 11.4.1 for a description of the use cases of traffic shaping and section 11.4.2 for the mechanisms of traffic shaping, such as rate limitation, spike smoothing and quotas.

11.2.3. Pagination

Especially collection resources can get quite big – too big for retrieving the entire collection in a single response. If it is not possible to return the complete collection due to its size, the collection may be chunked up, just like the search results from search engines. The bite-sized chunks of the collection resource are called pages. Each page contains a preset number of items, except if a custom page size is defined. The first page is returned right away, additional pages can be requested separately.

When should you use pagination? Implement pagination for large collection resources. For each call the API only has to collect, process and deliver the data of the page, not the data of the complete collection. In this way, pagination can improve the performance of the API.

And it also saves bandwidth and processing power for the client. This is especially important when developing APIs consumed by mobile apps. Your API consumers will love the fast response time of your API.

Pagination should be configurable via query parameters. To reach a specific page use the **page** query parameter. To change the number of items listed on one page use the **per_page** query parameter.

Here a pagination example of the Github API:

```
https://api.github.com/user/repos?page=3&per_page=100
```

To help the client navigate through the pages, the API may provide meta-information. On each page it includes links to reach other pages. This meta information can be transmitted in the link header, according to IETF RFC 5988 [29]. An example of such an HTTP header:

```
Link:
<https://api.github.com/user/repos?page=3&per_page=100>;rel="next",
<https://api.github.com/user/repos?page=50&per_page=100>;rel="last"
```

Alternatively, links to other pages can be included in the

HTTP body, as part of the JSON payload of each page. Each link can be annotated for its meaning using the INRIA link relation types:

- `self`: link to this page in the result set.
- `next`: link to the next page in the result set.
- `previous` or `prev`: link to the previous page.
- `first`: link to the next page in the result set.
- `last`: link to the next page in the result set.

Optionally, the following useful meta information for pagination can be included on each page:

- `pagesize` or `per_page`: the number of items on each page
- `totalpages`: the total number of pages for this data.
- `totalitems`: the total items returned over all pages.

11.2.4. Enable Content Compression

Content compression can be configured by the content negotiation mechanism of HTTP, using the `Content-Encoding` header. See section 7.3.2 for more information on content negotiation and content encoding.

11.2.5. Remove Whitespace from Responses

This mechanism for performance improvement is actually not recommended. It is sometimes stated, that performance can be improved by reducing white space from the HTTP body in JSON or XML, and that the response can be pretty-printed by the client.

In fact, it is not much that can be saved by whitespace removal. Repetitive whitespace is anyway eliminated by content compression (see sections 11.2.4 and 7.3.2). Even worse, by removing whitespace the understandability and intuitive discovery of the API gets hampered. Be aware of this tradeoff between performance and understandability of the API.

> Recommendation: Deliver API responses pretty printed and switch on content compression.

11.3. Caching

By storing frequently used data, caching can increase the performance of the API significantly. In the distributed system consisting of client app, API and backend, caching can be performed both by the client and by the API. We identify these common use cases in section 11.3.1. In section 11.3.2 we introduce the mechanisms for implementing caching and focus on the HTTP caching mechanism 11.3.3.

11.3.1. Use Cases for Caching

Caching can be performed client-side by the caller of the API. The API frontend needs to offer cache-friendly API responses. This option is studied in section 11.3.1.2. Alternatively, caching can be used in the API to store responses from the backend systems, see section 11.3.1.1.

11.3.1.1. API-Side Caching

In API-side caching, the API stores backend responses in a cache. On a cache hit, the backend response is immediately available from the cache without calling the backend. If the backend is RESTful, HTTP caching can be used (see next section), where the API takes on the role of the client. Alternatively simple time-based caches can be used for storing backend requests, depending on the requirements for freshness of the data.

11.3.1.2. Client-Side Caching

In client-side caching, the client stores the API responses in a cache on the client. In principle, client-side caching can be implemented using various caching mechanisms, such as time-based caching or HTTP caching. The advantage of client-side HTTP caching is, that it offers a protocol for cache control that ensures that the cached data is up to date.

11.3.1.3. What should be cached?

Not only positive responses (status code 2xx) should be cached, better overall application performance can be achieved by caching error responses as well. The approach is called "negative caching" and also includes 3xx and 4xx status codes, such as:

- `300 Multiple Choices`
- `301 Moved Permanently`
- `400 Bad Request`
- `403 Forbidden`
- `404 Not Found`
- `405 Method Not Allowed`
- `410 Gone`

11.3.2. Caching Mechanisms

To implement caching, you can choose from on a large number of existing caching mechanisms and algorithms. In a system designed according to the REST style, HTTP is used and the HTTP caching mechanism can be leveraged. HTTP caching is standardized and already implemented by HTTP-based infrastructure, such as HTTP servers and proxies.

11.3.3. HTTP Caching Mechanism with Conditional Requests

The advantages of the HTTP caching mechanism are that it is standardized and already implemented by HTTP-based infrastructure. Moreover, it offers a mechanism for cache control which ensures that the cached data is up to date. The mechanism is called conditional HTTP request. In general, the following steps are needed for sending conditional HTTP requests.

1. The client has the API response in cache with the URL and a token. The token is either the `ETag` header or the `Last-Modified-Date` header that was received with a previous API response. It identifies the version of the data that is cached.

2. The client sends a conditional request to the API. The client includes the token (identifying the currently cached version) via the appropriate HTTP header to the API. The API determines if the cached data is up to date (see section 11.3.3.1).

3. The API indicates if the cache is up to date and only processes the HTTP method if needed. This step is different for reading (see section 11.3.3.2) and writing access (see section 11.3.3.3).

11.3.3.1. Determining if the Cached Data is Up to Date

An advantages of HTTP based caching is its protocol for ensuring that the cached data is up to date. So how does the client determine in HTTP based caching if the cached data is up to date?

The client sends a regular (reading or writing) API request for the resource to the server and also identifies which version of the data is in the client-side cache. This identification is either based on `ETag` (see section 11.3.3.1) or based on `Last-Modified` (see section 11.3.3.1). If the API implements both methods, the client can chose which method to use. If the client uses both methods simultaneously, both conditions need to be checked.

ETag based Caching Client-side caching is implemented in HTTP using the `ETag: {etag-value}` HTTP header field. The API always includes an ETag in the response and sends it together with the requested resource to the client. ETags (Entity Tags) are hash values on the HTTP response that are computed by the API. The values are specific to a URL and the values change whenever the content of that URL changes. ETag values can be computed using a suitable hash algorithm or if a database is used, it can be automatically computed by a database (auto-increment a field on write).

The client stores the URL of the API together with ETag and the API response in a client-side cache. On the next request to the API, the client sets the HTTP header field `If-None-Match: {etag-value}` to the value of the cached ETag. The API checks the status of the ETag and returns an HTTP status code `304 Not Modified` if the resource was unchanged. This shows to the client that the cached value is up to date. The client can use the locally stored API response, making the interaction faster while also saving bandwidth. If the ETag does not match, the API sends its response as usual and also returns the new ETag

225

value in the ETag header field.

Last-Modified based Caching An alternative implementation relies on the Last-Modified date instead of the ETag value to identify the latest version in the cache. The client stores the URL of the API together with the Last-Modified date and the API response in a client-side cache. On the next request to the API, the client sets the value of the HTTP header field `If-Unmodified-Since` to the date stored in the cache. The API compares the date from the `If-Unmodified-Since` header against the last modification date on the API. The API either sends a `304 Not Modified` or the usual API response is computed and returned with an updated `Last-Modified` header.

11.3.3.2. Reading Cached Data with Conditional GET

The following steps are needed to read cached data with a conditional GET:

1. The client has the API response in cache with the URL and a token. The token is either the `ETag` header or the `Last-Modified-Date` header that was received with a previous API response. It identifies the version of the data.

2. The client attempts to read with a conditional GET. The client sends the token (identifying the currently cached version) via appropriate HTTP header. In case of an `ETag` token, it is sent in the `If-None-Match` header, in case of the `Last-Modified` token, it is sent in the HTTP header `If-Unmodified-Since`.

3. API returns an HTTP status code `304 Not Modified` if the resource was unchanged. It delivers the resource as usual if the token is invalid.

11.3.3.3. Writing Cached Data with Conditional PUT and DELETE

Potential integrity problems with PUT and DELETE are lost updates and stale deletes. For PUT or DELETE the cache control works in a similar manner as for GET. The client includes the header `If-Match: {etag-value}` or `If-Unmodified-Since: {date}`, containing the value/date of the last request. In case the value is not up to date any more, the HTTP status code `412 Precondition Failed` is sent, otherwise the PUT or DELETE succeeds. It works as follows:

1. The client has the API response in cache with the URL and a token. The token is either the `ETag` header or the `Last-Modified-Date` header that was received with a previous API response. It identifies the version of the data.

2. The client attempts to write with a conditional PUT or DELETE. The client sends the token (identifying the currently cached version) via appropriate HTTP header. In case of an `ETag` token, it is sent in the HTTP header `If-Match`, in case of a `Last-Modified` token, it is sent in the HTTP header `If-Unmodified-Since`.

3. The API delivers a success if the token is still valid and fails if the token is invalid. The API might also fail if no token was provided.

This mechanism can be used with writing access via PUT and DELETE. To prevent lost updates, the API may require a token (obtained in step 1) and refuse to perform any writing access without the token in step 2. In this case the API should send status codes `428 Precondition Required`, as specified in IETF RFC 6585 [28].

11.3.3.4. Cache-Control

It is possible to fine-tune and configure the behavior of caching depending on the particular needs of the API consumer. The cache-control mechanism offers these possibilities.

Switching Caching Off Clients should be able to overwrite the caching implemented by the API by adding the HTTP header parameters `Cache-Control: no-cache`. If these parameters are supplied, the API always returns the latest value and not the cached value.

Header Parameters for Cache Control There are several HTTP header fields to control, improve and fine-tune caching. These are `Cache-Control, Last-Modified, Date` and `ETag`.

- The `Cache-Control` header field is set by the API and is the main control for caching. It allows setting several directives:

    - The `max-age {value}` directive indicates that caches can hold cached values for max-age seconds. Example: `Cache-Control: max-age=3600`

    - The `no-cache` directive or no-store directive indicates that no caching should be performed on this resources. Example: `Cache-Control: no-cache`

    - The `public` directive indicates that no caching should be performed. Example: `Cache-Control: public`

    - The `private` directive indicates that no caching should be performed. Example: `Cache-Control: private`

    - The `must-revalidate` directive indicates that the server must be checked for each request. Example: `Cache-Control: must-revalidate`

- The `Date` header field is set by the API and indicates when the response was sent and helps clients to compute the refresh time.

- The `Last-Modified` header field is set by the API and indicates when the resource was last changed and helps clients to determine the freshness of the cached data.

- The `ETag` header field is set by the API and is a hash of the content and thus changes when the content changes. It can be used by clients to determine the freshness of the cached data.

- The `Expires` header field is set by the API and indicates the date at which the cached value expires. It is only used for backward compatibility with HTTP 1.0. In HTTP 1.1 it is replaced by the `Date` and `Cache-Control: max-age` header fields.

Limitations of Cache-Control The cache-control logic of HTTP works well if the resource can exclusively be updated via HTTP. E.g. the cache is invalidated when there is a PUT of the resource. However, if the backend systems can be updated by other means, for example by writing directly to the database or by an internal app or process not using the API, the cached resource might be stale. Advanced options are cache channels, that the cache can subscribe to, in order to get triggered on an update by the backend.

11.4. Traffic Shaping

Traffic shaping can be used to guarantee a minimum level of performance for all consumers, even if the load on the API is pretty high. When traffic shaping is configured correctly, it can be avoided that one API consumer cannibalizes the system.

Traffic shaping ensures that the traffic does not grow out of control and threaten the availability of the API and the availability of the backend. The goal is to ensure or guarantee a certain performance availability, even under heavy load. For this goal it is important to protect the API platform and the backends from overload. It allows us to guarantee and enforce SLAs for APIs and minimize latency for apps. At the same time, traffic shaping protects from attacks, such as denial of service attacks (DOS) or from buggy apps that bombard the API due to a software error.

In section 11.4.1 we identify common use cases for traffic shaping and in section 11.4.2 we introduce the mechanisms for implementing traffic shaping.

11.4.1. Use Cases for Traffic Shaping

Traffic shaping can be applied on inbound connections to the API or on outbound connections to the backends. Traffic shaping on inbound connections protects the API platform as a whole. Traffic shaping on outbound connections protects specific backend systems.

11.4.1.1. Use Case: Protect API Platform

If traffic shaping is used to protect the API platform, the complete inbound traffic to the API platform needs to be limited or shaped. To protect the availability of the API platform, it is not relevant, which consumer caused the traffic.

11.4.1.2. Use Case: Protect Backends

If traffic shaping is used to protect the backends, the outbound traffic to each backend has to be limited or shaped, no matter which consumer caused it or from which API the traffic originates. Backends have a limited capacity, as they have not been designed and dimensioned for heavy traffic. Moreover, the backend systems may not offer the traffic shaping mechanisms for protecting themselves from high traffic volumes. To ensure the availability of the backend system, the API has to protect the backend.

11.4.1.3. Use Case: Limit User Access

For this use case the traffic originating from a specific API consumer needs to be limited and shaped. This helps to ensure that there is not a single user that dominates the system, uses up its resources and makes it effectively unavailable to other users.

If both authenticated and unauthenticated users can access a public API, it is a typical approach to distinguish between authenticated and unauthenticated users and grant higher limits to authenticated users. How do we identify unauthenticated users? We identify them by their IP address.

11.4.2. Mechanisms for Traffic Shaping

Traffic shaping allows for controlling the traffic that is received by the API platform or the traffic that is sent to a backend. Traffic shaping is implemented by delaying traffic: We can limit the maximum rate at which the traffic is sent (see section 11.4.2.1 on rate limitation), we can limit the volume of traffic that is sent (see section 11.4.2.3 on quota), or we can control the traffic patterns (see section 11.4.2.2 on spike limitation and spike smoothing).

11.4.2.1. Rate Limitation

Rate limitation is a form of traffic shaping in which the maximum number of API requests per time window is limited. Rate limitation is an appropriate mechanism for the use case of protecting the API (use case 11.4.1.1) and for the use case of protecting the backends (use case 11.4.1.2). The relevant parameters for implementing rate limitation are:

- A time window, during which we limit the requests.
- A counter of the requests in the current time window.
- A maximum number of requests allowed per time window.

If the counter exceeds the maximum, further requests in the time window are either rejected or throttled down (= delayed) to an acceptable rate. If the requests shall be throttled, they are put into a queue for later processing. The queue has a fixed length, offering space for a certain number of requests. If the queue is full, requests are rejected. To smooth out the stored requests in the queue, the algorithm waits for some time, and schedules one request from the queue for processing. The algorithm continues until the queue is empty.

For rejected calls, return status code `429 Too Many Requests` and an appropriate error message, when the rate limit is exceeded. Unlike most other status codes we recommend to use, 429 is not specified in the HTTP 1.1 spec, instead it is specified in IETF RFC 6585 [28].

Instead of surprising the consumer with a sudden status code 429, it is good style to inform the consumer already before hitting the rate limit. It is common practice to include current rate information into each HTTP header sent by the API. Twitter for example uses the following HTTP headers (`https://dev.twitter.com/docs/rate-limiting/1.1`):

- `XRateLimitLimit` header: maximum number of requests allowed in the current time window.
- `XRateLimitRemaining` header: remaining number of requests allowed in the current time window.
- `XRateLimitReset` header: remaining time in the current time window.

Optimistic Rate Limitation Checking rate limits can be expensive – and in some use cases it may not even be necessary. Instead of checking the rate limits on every request in real time, you can decide to trust the callers for a whole day, but log the usage. At the end of the day you count up how many requests they made and block those consumers who have exceeded their quotas. The advantage of this approach is that the synchronous calculations are kept to a minimum and the remaining calculations can be performed asynchronously.

Optimistic rate limiting attempts to "educate" the callers of the API. It does, however, not protect the systems from overload in real time.

11.4.2.2. Spike Limitation and Spike Smoothing

Spike limitation protects against sudden traffic spikes (or traffic bursts). It can be used to protect the API (use case 11.4.1.1) or to protect the backends (use case 11.4.1.2). The traffic spikes may be caused by DOS attacks, by a sudden popularity of the API (slashdot effect) or by a mere coincidence.

To realize spike limitation, you need to maintain the timestamp of the last request and you need to predefine a minimum interval between consecutive requests. If a request arrives already before the minimum interval has passed, it is rejected with a `429 Too Many Requests` status code.

Spike smoothing is a variant of spike limitation. To realize spike smoothing, the timestamp of the last request and the minimum interval are needed, in addition to a fixed-length request queue. Requests during a traffic spike are put into a queue for later processing. The queue has a fixed length, offering space for a certain number of requests. If the queue is full, requests are rejected with a `429 Too Many Requests` status code. To smooth out the stored requests in the queue, the algorithm waits for the minimum time interval to pass, and schedules one request from the queue for processing. The algorithm continues until the queue is empty.

When setting up spike limitation and spike smoothing, it is essential to fine-tune the parameters and find the correct minimum interval between consecutive requests. This value is typically determined based on experience with the system and based on experimentation.

11.4.2.3. Traffic Shaping with Quota

The quota mechanism is typically used to limit the API traffic of a specific consumer to a certain number of requests or to a certain transfer volume per time window (use case 11.4.1.3).

To realize the quota, three variables need to be defined: a counter, a time window and a limit. The counter is reset periodically at the beginning of a new time window. The counter is increase on each request. All requests are processed until the counter exceeds the limit, in which case the API fails with a **429 Too Many Requests**.

The mechanism for realizing the quota is similar to the mechanism of rate limitation: a certain number of requests is allowed per time window. The time window, however, is usually much longer for quotas, e.g. a month, whereas the time window for rate limitation is typically very short, e.g. one second.

Of course the consumer needs to be identified. It can be done via the security mechanisms API key, HTTP basic, HTTP digest, OAuth Token or JWT (see section 11.1.3), and in case of an unauthenticated user the IP address would need to be used.

11.5. Evolution and Versioning

> Successful software always gets changed.
>
> *Frederick P. Brooks*

11.5.1. The Evolution Challenge

Managing change in software systems is never easy, but it is especially difficult to manage change in loosely-coupled distributed systems, such as API solutions. In loosely-coupled distributed systems not only the software components themselves are distributed, but also the responsibilities of the different components are distributed over different organizations, companies and people.

The API provider has little control over the client implementations of the consumer that use the API. The API provider might not even know all applications of the consumer, which call the API. This means that an unknown number of unidentified software components might rely on the API.

Already a small change in the API is enough to break some of the clients consuming the API. From the perspective of the API consumer, longevity and stability are important aspects of published APIs. The simple rule is, that the externally observable behavior of an API (from the perspective of the clients) cannot be changed, once the API has been published.

If the interface of the API changes anyway, it is impossible for the API provider to change all the apps consuming the API, and it is equally impractical to force all consumers to adapt or update their apps. API consumers are typically not willing and not interested in dealing with APIs that change frequently and will quickly abandon APIs that force them to rewrite their app.

11.5.2. Publication: The Root Cause of the Evolution Challenge

The root cause for the evolution challenge is the publication of the API. Once the API has been published, any externally observable behavior of the API cannot be changed without breaking clients.

The restriction imposed by this rule might sound severe and even counter-intuitive, since APIs are often developed using an agile development approach. Agile approaches are based on feedback loops and the idea of many incremental changes of the software. The agile development approach still applies to new or unpublished APIs.

However, as soon as APIs are published, the game changes. When APIs are published, they become available for consumers and it has to be assumed that the consumers build apps with the APIs. Published APIs cannot be changed in an agile manner. At least, APIs need to stay backward (and forward) compatible, so that old clients do not break and new clients can use the new and improved features.

11.5.3. Types of API Evolution

People may want to change various aspects of published APIs. Are all of these changes equally severe for the clients? In this section we analyze potential changes and classify them according to their severity. Severe changes are those changes that are incompatible (see section 11.5.3.2) and break a client. Not so severe are those API changes, that do not impact the client. They are called backward compatible (see section 11.5.3.1).

11.5.3.1. Backward Compatible Changes

An API is backward compatible if an unchanged client can interact with a changed API. The unchanged client should be able to use all the functionality that was offered by the old API.

If a change is supposed to be backward compatible, certain changes to the API are prohibited, others are possible. The following is a list of backward compatible changes:

- Adding query parameters (they should always be optional).
- Adding header or form parameters, as long as they are optional.
- Adding new fields in JSON or XML data structures, as long as they are optional.
- Adding endpoints, e.g. a new REST resource.
- Adding operations to an existing endpoint, e.g. when using SOAP.
- Adding optional fields to the request interfaces.
- Changing mandatory fields to optional fields in an existing API.

11.5.3.2. Incompatible Changes

If a change to the API breaks the client, the change was incompatible. In general, removing and changing aspects of the API leads to incompatibilities. A non-exhaustive list of incompatible changes:

- Removing or changing data structures, i.e. by changing, removing, or redefining fields in the data structure.
- Removing fields from the request or response (as opposed to making it optional).
- Changing a previously optional request field in the body or parameter into a mandatory field.

- Changing a previously required response field in the body or parameter into an optional field.

- Changing the URI of the API, such as host name, port or path.

- Changing the structure or relationship between request or response fields, e.g. making an existing field a child of some other field.

- Adding a new mandatory field to the data structure.

Incompatible changes should be avoided if possible. If the change needs to be made, a new, additional version of the API has to be created, which exists in parallel to the existing API version.

11.5.3.3. Conclusion of the Analysis

Compatible changes can be implemented with an in place update, the client does not break and no new version needs to be created. Incompatible changes would break the client and thus need to be offered as a new version. A recommendation is to perform only non-breaking, i.e. additive changes.

11.5.4. Anticipating and Avoiding Evolution

Since evolution is difficult to manage, APIs should ideally be built in such a manner, that evolution becomes practically unnecessary and that any foreseeable changes can be realized as compatible changes. This is, however, not always possible, because changes cannot always be anticipated.

The next best approach to anticipating changes is a mature development process. A mature development process may be able to avoid evolution to some extent. The need for evolution can be reduced by eliminating some of the most common causes for evolution. Evolution becomes necessary if the API has been published prematurely. From a business perspective, there are forces to publish as early as possible. From an long term support perspective, there are forces to publish as late as possible, to avoid evolution cycles. Good results can be achieved by compromising between both forces. This can be done by working closely with 1-2 pilot consumers of the API.

11.5.5. Coping with Evolution - Versioning

If evolution cannot be avoided by anticipating or avoiding changes we need to cope with the change. For this purpose, we need to study the change more closely: Is it a compatible or an incompatible change?

Compatible changes do not break the clients. They should be reflected by a new minor version, which is fully compatible with the previous version.

Incompatible changes to published interfaces will break all clients. Incompatible changes need to be implemented in such a way that existing clients are not affected. This can be accomplished by creating a new major version of the API and maintaining the unchanged API alongside the changed API. Creating and publishing a new version of the API is overhead and thus slows down any changes to the API. Moreover, major versions need to be visible to the consumers and they need to be accessible by the consumers. There are different techniques for making major versions accessible, as discussed in the following sections.

11.5.5.1. Realize API Versioning in Accept Header

The client can use the HTTP `Accept` header to explicitly indicate the version of the API. The `Accept` header still contains the MIME-types as usual, but in addition the version is appended. The URI of the API does not contain any version information. For new versions, the URL does not change, but the request header.

```
Accept: application/json; version=1
```

It is recommended not to introduce a default version. Without any default version, clients are required to always specify the version they expect and can deal with. This type of mandatory versioning requires that versioning is introduced right from the start, when the first version of the API is published.

This versioning concept in the Accept header may be extended further. The extension offers the possibility to version two aspects of the API separately: the API (version 5 in the example) and the JSON schema (version 3 in the example):

```
Accept: com.domain.v3.application/json; version=5
```

11.5.5.2. Realize API Versioning as URI Path Parameter

The most common technique for versioning uses a URI parameter with the version number. For example:

```
https://domain.com/v1/API
```

Advantages of this approach are the widespread use and the browser compatibility. Different versions can be explored via browser.

11.5.5.3. Realize API Versioning in a Custom HTTP Header

A custom HTTP header could be defined for the version. For example `X-Version: 1.1`

In general, the use of custom HTTP headers is not recommended. This approach can lead to problems with caching. This approach is not recommended.

11.5.5.4. Realize API Versioning as Query Parameter

A query parameter could be defined for the version. For example:

```
https://domain.com/API?version=1
```

This approach is not recommended.

11.5.5.5. Realize API Versioning as a new Subdomain

A subdomain could be defined for the new version. For example:

```
https://v1.domain.com/API
```

This approach is not recommended.

11.5.5.6. HATEOAS Versioning via Links

Hypermedia solves the versioning issue by indirection via a link resource. A link resource is comparable to a pointer in the C programming language or a symbolic link in the file system. A link resource has a separate identity and a separate URI from the versioned resource that it points to. The resource that it points to still needs to be versioned using e.g. the URI Path (see section 11.5.5.2). But the link resource is not versioned. The link resource is updated to always point to the latest version of the versioned resource. The only address that is communicated to the client is the URI of the link resource, whose address never changes. In this way, the HATEOAS style can provide a solution for the evolution problem.

How can the linking be implemented? Well, there are several options. For example via an HTTP redirect (301 or 302) with the URI of the versioned API in the HTTP `Location` header. Another option is including the URI of the versioned resource into the payload of the link resource.

11.5.6. Supporting Multiple Versions Simultaneously

You have versioned your API and you are ready to share the new major version with the world? Great! But what to do with the old version?

You may keep the old version of the API running, at least for a certain grace period. Notify your consumers and convince them of the benefits of the new version. Engaged consumers will eventually switch to the new version.

Keeping the old version of the API running is another option, but a costly one: infrastructure, monitoring, support and documentation have to be provided for all active versions. Providing several versions may also confuse new API consumers looking for documentation. So eventually old versions should be retired and switched off. You will have to live with the fact, that some consumers will not make the switch to the new version of the API.

12. API Client Design

The design of API clients is not within the scope of this book. But API client design helps us to see our API from the perspective of the API consumer. By understanding the perspective of the API consumer and her challenges, we put ourselves into the shoes of the API customer (see chapter 2 on consumer-oriented API design). From this perspective of the API consumer we should review and check our API design.

What is the most effective way to check our API design? We eat our own dog food! After having designed an API, we build a client that consumes our API. We choose a realistic use case for your API and implement that use case. Let's find out whether we would choose our own API over existing third party APIs (see section12.1), whether we can easily discover our API (see section 12.2) and whether we can easily call our API (see section 12.3).

If we find anything that is painful, complicated or unclear about the API from the consumer's perspective, we should consider redesigning our API.

12.1. Designing the Solution

We first need to design the overall solution, which includes both the API and a client for that API. We need to identify the functionality of the solution and assign this functionality to either the API or to the client (see section 12.1.1). This helps us to review if the API solves an appropriate problem.

When building a client, the API consumer needs to decide if a new API should to be built, or if the functionality is already covered by an existing API (see section 12.1.2). This step allows us to identify what is unique about our API and how the functionality of our API compares to the competition on the market.

And in the latter case, we need to know how to choose an existing API (see section 12.1.3). This step allows us to review the marketing of our API and how our API can be found by potential API consumers.

12.1.1. Functionality in the Client or in the API?

Let's assume that our API-based solution consists of an API and a mobile app as API client. Despite great app development frameworks, not all functionality can and should be realized natively in the app. Typical functionality that cannot be realized inside the app includes:

- Access to real time data
- Access to data bases and large file sets
- Access to remote sensor data (e.g. for IoT devices)
- Access to proprietary algorithms
- Heavy computation or number crunching (e.g. speech recognition)
- Persistent storage of data (e.g. for realizing omni-channel experiences across several devices)

The above functionality is typically realized on the server, exposed in the form of an API and called from the API client. If an API deals with one of the above functionalities, it solves a problem that is appropriate for APIs.

12.1.2. Use an existing API or build a new API?

The design of the API client includes the choice of the API. The API consumer has the choice to use an existing API (and pay for its use) or to build a new API. When given the choice, API consumers typically prefer to just use an API that has already been developed and tested. This allows API consumers to integrate the API quickly and focus on adding value on top with their app.

If the required API already exists, the API client can be built quickly. The API consumer needs to register her client with the API provider to receive credentials, set up the payment for the usage of the API and integrate the API with the client. The important steps for choosing a third party API are outlined in the next section.

Often, however, none of the existing APIs fits the requirements exactly. A completely new API needs to be developed. The API may be developed by a third party API provider or by the API consumer. If the API is developed by the API consumer, the API consumer also becomes an API provider.

12.1.3. How to choose a third party API?

When integrating a third party API, the API consumer needs to be able to (1) find the API, (2) test the API, (3) use the API and (4) learn about the API provider. For a quick integration and a positive developer experience, it is essential, that these four steps are as smooth as possible for the API consumer.

12.1.3.1. Step 1: Find and Discovering the API

There is a global market for third-party APIs. The API consumer chooses from the APIs offered on this market. An overview of the market is available in the yellow pages for APIs or on

245

market places for APIs. See section 12.2 for more details on this step.

When we review our API, we need to find out if our API is listed in the yellow pages if it is available on all the relevant market places and if it can be found easily when searching with keywords or categories.

12.1.3.2. Step 2: Test the API

Once the API has been found on the market, consumers want to learn more about the API. When learning about APIs, consumers prefer to test the API, see examples for calling the API and only if they have done the first things they are willing to read the documentation of the API. Interactive documentation provides all the above things, especially testing the API.

API consumers typically want to test the API before committing to its use in order to confirm that it satisfies both runtime aspects and development aspects of the overall requirements. Runtime aspects comprise the functional requirements and the non-functional requirements of the API, such as stability, longevity, performance and security. The development aspects comprise the relationship between API provider and the developers of the API consumer.

The development aspect might be more important than it seems, since the developers of the API consumer are in fact the only people who interact with the API directly. So what do the developers of the API consumers look for? API consumers look for APIs with a great community, great support, great documentation and tools that will make client development and operation as smooth and as simple as possible. And ideally, the engagement platform makes it easy to get a taste the API via an interactive documentation.

12.1.3.3. Step 3: Use the API and Learn about the API

API consumers want to access the API documentation, register for the API, obtain their credentials and choose an appropriate payment plan. APIs are typically sold as services, i.e. the API consumer needs to pay for the usage of the API. Various payment plans may be available, e.g. payment by the number of calls, by the number of days, or by the consumed bandwidth. These payment plans should be available and clearly understandable.

Access to documentation, registration for new credentials and the sign up for payment plans should be as smooth and as simple as possible. Engagement platforms typically provide generated (potentially interactive) documentation and a self-service interface for obtaining credentials, such as client IDs or API keys.

12.1.3.4. Step 4: Learn about the API Provider

Once APIs are integrated into apps, they often turn out to be essential and central components of the app. Apps will cease to work properly when the API is unavailable. This is why the API consumer needs to trust the providers of the APIs they use.

API consumers may worry about the API provider not being around any longer, the API the API being terminated or being changed. This is why API consumers are interested in the stability and longevity of the API. When choosing an API, consumers should evaluate both the stability of the API provider as a company and the stability of the API from a technical perspective.

A hint for the stability of the API provider is a sound business model. Providing APIs needs to make business sense for the provider. This is why paid APIs are typically considered "safer" and more stable. Keeping alive paid APIs is in the self-interest of the API provider, so API provider and API consumer are aligned.

A hint for the stability of the API is provided by the history of the API. Has the API been changed? Are new versions deployed? Are old versions still supported? Is the phase-out at the end of the API life cycle described in the terms of service?

12.2. Discovering APIs

An API first needs to be discovered. It can be discovered manually by potential API consumers or automatically by discovery algorithms.

For API consumers, discovery is all about finding an API that solves a problem they have in the context of their app. For API providers, discovery offers the opportunity for promoting their API effectively.

12.2.1. Consumer Discovery

There is a global market for third-party APIs. The API consumer chooses from the APIs offered on this market. An overview of the market is available via

- Search engine for APIs (e.g. `http://apis.io`)

- Yellow pages for APIs (e.g. `http://programmableweb.com`)

- Market places for APIs (e.g. `http://mashape.com`)

In a human-centered discovery approach, APIs are discovered based on their description on the market place and on the engagement platform. Developers need to search for and discover the API while designing their solution or API client. The approach is thus also known as design-time discovery.

12.2.2. Automatic Discovery

Besides manual discovery by humans, APIs could also be discovered automatically by machines. Automatic discovery is also known as runtime discovery. For SOAP services, a range of standards such as WSDL, UDDI provide pieces for automatic web-service discovery.

For RESTful APIs, such sophisticated standards for automated discover do not exist, yet. Here is a proposal for automated discovery of RESTful APIs:

1. In a first step of discovery, the URL of the resource needs to be discovered, e.g. via HATEOAS or via API yellow pages. To find an API and its URL via API yellow pages (e.g. `http://programmableweb.com`) the discovery program searches the directory of the yellow pages for annotations or keywords. To find an API via HATEOAS, the discovery program first accesses the root resource of the API provider to get a listing of all APIs. This listing needs to contain some meta-information, such as keywords, which can be used to identify the desired API and its URL. For this purpose, the discovery program needs to parse the syntax and understand the semantics of the API listings it receives.

2. In the second step of discovery, the methods that can be called on the resources need to be identified. Invoking the HTTP method OPTIONS on a given resource may provide this information. In a basic implementation the response is status code `204 No Content` with the HTTP header field `Allow`, containing a comma separated list of HTTP methods, which are used with this resource. A more advanced implementation of the OPTIONS method delivers an API description, e.g. in RAML or Swagger. By specifying the desired format in the `Accept` header,

the API may deliver different representations of the API description, e.g. WADL, RAML, Swagger and a HTML documentation.

12.3. Calling APIs

An API client, or API stub, is a small infrastructure component of the app, which handles the interaction with the API. An API client has two responsibilities: it needs to prepare & send the API request (see section 12.3.1) and process the API response (see section 12.3.2).

Attempting to call the API can provide valuable feedback for the API design. If you for example experience some difficulties in creating the API request or in parsing the API response, the API design is not consumer-friendly, yet. In this case, consider a redesign of the API.

The design approach proposed in this book (see chapter 4) is built around an API description. The API description does not only support the design of the API itself, but also the design of the API client. With an API description it is relatively simple and straightforward to call APIs: Client stubs can be generated automatically for any major programming language based on the API description. Alternatively, the API description can be manually translated into an API call.

12.3.1. Prepare and Send the API Request

Clients should call APIs only via the HTTPS protocol. Unencrypted HTTP traffic is not secure and should be avoided. In their request, clients should supply a unique transaction identifier in the request (see section 11.1), to allow for consistent logging. Depending on the security mechanism (see section 11.1), an API key, an OAuth token, or username/password should be provided.

With the API call, clients start the content negotiation. Since clients need to be able to process the results provided by the API, they need to make some assumptions about the representation. It is best if the clients clearly indicate their assumptions and negotiate the representation format. As part of every API call, clients should send the list of the representations they can process via the `Accept` header. Several accept headers are used for the preferred language, encoding, compression or content-type. See section 7.3.4 on content negotiation for more details. It is always good if the client explicitly indicates the preferences for the representation, since the API might change its default representation.

12.3.2. Process the API Response

Clients should process the representation permissively. In case of syntactic errors in the response, the client should not simply throw an error, but should attempt to interpret and use the available information as much as possible. An example of permissive processing is a web browser that will even render malformed HTML rather than displaying a blank page.

When APIs return an error status code, the client has to react appropriately. For a list of typical, standardized status codes, see section 7.6 and appendix E.

In general, for 4xx status codes, the client has to fix something in the request and try again. For idempotent HTTP methods, such as a GET, PUT or DELETE, this can be done without further precautions. For all non-idempotent methods, namely the POST method, a consistency check should be performed by the client, before retrying.

All 5xx status codes indicate a server error. The client does not need to take any precautions in that case and can try again later. The retry time should be indicated in the error message or by the `Retry-After` header field in the response.

The following list is a rough guideline for client's behavior in case of an API error. The list is indexed by the status code.

- **400 Bad Request**: Check the error description in the payload of the response for details. Correct the request and try again.

- **401 Not Authorized**: Check your credentials and if the authentication method used is supported by the API. Supply correct credentials and try again.

- **402 Insufficient Funds**: Top up your current price plan and retry.

- **403 Not Allowed**: The client does not have the rights to access the resource. Request the rights or use a different user account with sufficient rights. Then retry the request.

- **404 Not Found**: The resource is not available, correct the URL and retry.

- **405 Method Not Allowed**: The supplied HTTP verb is not available for the supplied resource. Check the `Allow` header to get the available HTTP verbs on the requested resource. Alternatively use the OPTIONS verb on the resource, to get a listing of all available HTTP verbs for this resource.

- **406 Not Acceptable**: None of the media-types acceptable by the client can be supplied by the API. Send a different `Accept` header and retry.

- **409 Conflict**: Check the error description in the payload of the response for details.

- **410 Gone**: The resource is not available any longer, check the URL.

- **412 Precondition Failed**: Stale Cache. Update the cache and try again.

- **413 Payload Too Large**: The payload is too large. Resend with a smaller payload. Check the error description of the response for further details.

- **415 Unsupported Media Type**: The content type of the payload sent from client to the API is not supported by the API. Check the API documentation for acceptable media-types. Resend the request with a supported media-type.

- **429 Too Many Requests**: The server is overloaded with too many requests. Check the `Retry-After` header to determine when to try the request again.

- **500 Server Error**: Log the error. Could be an instable server implementation. Check the `Retry-After` header to determine when to try the request again.

- **503 Service Unavailable**: Check the `Retry-After` header to determine when to try the request again.

A. Appendix

A.1. Feedback

If you enjoyed this book and got some value from it, it would be great if you could share with others what you liked about the book on the Amazon review page.

If you feel something was missing or you are not satisfied with your purchase, please contact me at matt@api-university.com. I read this email personally and am very interested in your feedback.

A.2. About the Author

Matthias has provided expertise to international and national companies on software architecture, software development processes and software integration. At some point he got a PhD.

Nowadays, Matthias uses his background in software engineering to help companies to realize their digital transformation agenda and to bring innovative software solutions to the market.

He also loves sharing his knowledge in the classroom, at workshops and in his books. Matthias is an instructor at the API-University, publishes a blog on APIs, is author of several books on APIs and regularly speaks at technology conferences.

A.3. Other Products by the Author

A.3.1. Online Course on RESTful API Design

Looking for best practices of RESTful API Design? This course is for you! Why? This course provides interactive video tutorials on the best practices of RESTful design. These best practices are based on the lessons learned from building and designing APIs over many years.

The course also includes video lectures on technical aspects of RESTful API Design, including the correct use of resources, URIs, representations, content-types, data formats, parameters, HTTP status codes and HTTP methods. And thanks to many interactive quizzes, learning REST becomes an engaging and exciting game-like experience.

We focus on the practical application of the knowledge, to get you ready for your first RESTful API project. The course includes guided mini-projects to get you ready for the practical application of REST.

After completing this course, you will be able to design RESTful APIs – but not just any APIs, you have all the knowledge to design APIs, which your consumers will love.

Title: RESTful API Design

Lecturer: Matthias Biehl

Release Date: 2016-09-30

Material: Video, Workbooks, Quizzes

Length: 3h

http://api-university.com/courses/restful-api-design-course

A.3.2. Book on API Architecture

Looking for the big picture of building APIs? This book is for you!

Building APIs that consumers love should certainly be the goal of any API initiative. However, it is easier said than done. It requires getting the architecture for your APIs right. This book equips you with both foundations and best practices for API architecture. This book presents best practices for putting an infrastructure in place that enables efficient development of APIs. This book is for you if you want to understand the big picture of API design and development, you want to define an API architecture, establish a platform for APIs or simply want to build APIs your consumers love. What is API architecture? Architecture spans the bigger picture of APIs and can be seen from several perspectives: The architecture of the complete solution, the technical architecture of the API platform, the architecture of the API portfolio, the design decisions for a particular API proxy. This book covers all of the above perspectives on API architecture. However, to become useful, the architecture needs to be put into practice. This is why§ this book covers an API methodology for design and development. An API methodology provides practical guidelines for putting API architecture into practice. It explains how to develop an API architecture into an API that consumers love.

Title: API Architecture
Author: Matthias Biehl
Release Date: 2015-05-22
Length: 190 pages
ISBN-13: 978-1508676645

http://api-university.com/books/api-architecture

A.3.3. Online Course on API Security with OAuth 2.0

Securing APIs is complicated? This course offers an introduction to API Security with OAuth 2.0. In 3 hours you will gain an overview of the capabilities of OAuth. You will learn the core concepts of OAuth. You will get to know all 4 OAuth flows that are used in cloud solutions and mobile apps. You will also be able to look over the shoulder of an expert using OAuth for the APIs of Facebook, LinkedIn, Google and Paypal.

Title: OAuth 2.0 - Getting Started in Web-API Security
Lecturer: Matthias Biehl
Release Date: 2015-07-30
Material: Video, Workbooks, Quizzes
Length: 4h

http://api-university.com/courses/oauth-2-0-course

A.3.4. Book on API Security with OAuth 2.0

This book offers an introduction to API Security with OAuth 2.0. In less than 80 pages you will gain an overview of the capabilities of OAuth. You will learn the core concepts of OAuth. You will get to know all 4 OAuth Flows that are used in cloud solutions and mobile apps. If you have tried to read the official OAuth specification, you may get the impression that OAuth is complicated. This book explains OAuth in simple terms. The different OAuth Flows are visualized graphically using sequence diagrams. The diagrams allow you to see the big picture of the various OAuth interactions. This high-level overview is complemented with a rich set of example requests and responses and an explanation of the technical details. In the book the challenges and benefits of OAuth are presented, followed by an explanation of the technical concepts of OAuth. The technical concepts include the actors, endpoints, tokens and the four OAuth flows. Each flow is described in detail, including the use cases for each flow. Extensions of OAuth - so called profiles - are presented, such as OpenID Connect and the SAML2 Bearer Profile. Sequence diagrams are presented to explain the necessary interactions.

Title: OAuth 2.0 - Getting Started in Web-API Security
Author: Matthias Biehl
Release Date: 2014-11-15
Length: 76 pages
ISBN-13: 978-1507800911

http://api-university.com/books/oauth-2-0-book

B. Typical Content-Types

There is also a large list of standardized MIME-types, maintained by IANA [24]. In addition, custom content-types can be defined, for example: If you need to define your own content-type and want to make it publicly available, follow IETF RFC 6838 [25].

List of typically used content-types:

- application/x-www-form-urlencoded: to send data as form parameters with the POST method.

- multipart/form-data: to send generic data, such as a file or binary data, with the POST method.

- application/json: to send JSON data.

- application/schema+json: to send JSON Schema.

- application/merge-patch+json: to express the difference between two JSON data structures, use JSON Merge-Patch, IETF RFC 7396 [35].

- application/xml: to send XML data.

- application/raml+yaml: to send RAML descriptions.

- application/openapi+json: to send OpenAPI/Swagger descriptions (proposed).

C. HTTP Methods

List of HTTP methods:

- CONNECT: method for establishing a tunnel; method is not safe and not idempotent.

- DELETE: method for removal of a resource; method is not safe but idempotent.

- GET: method for retrieval of a resource in the selected representation; method is safe, and idempotent.

- HEAD: same behavior as GET but without payload; method is safe and idempotent.

- OPTIONS: method for requesting details about the supported methods for the specified resource; method is safe and idempotent.

- POST: method for sending enclosed payload to the server for creation, appending or processing; method is not safe and not idempotent.

- PUT: method for replacing or creating the resource with the enclosed payload; method is not safe but idempotent.

- PATCH: method for selectively modifying parts of an existing resource; method is not safe and not idempotent.

- TRACE: method for connection testing, the recipient should reflect the message in the message body; method is safe and idempotent.

D. HTTP Headers

Generic Header Parameters

- `Content-Type`: specifies the syntax and semantics of the HTTP body. The content-type is also called media-type or MIME-type.

- `Content-Length`: specifies the length of the content in bytes: It allows the recipient to check if she has read the complete content.

- `Content-Language`: specifies the language of the representation, using a two-letter code according to IETF RFC 5646 [11].

- `Content-Location`: specifies the address at which the content of the HTTP body can be retrieved with a GET. It indicates that the HTTP body contains a copy of the resource, whose address is given in the `Content-Location` header.

- `Content-Encoding`: specifies the compression method used. Allowed values are `gzip`, `compress` or `deflate`.

- `Content-MD5`: contains a hash/digest of the content to check the integrity.

- `Date`: a timestamp when the request was sent.

- `Host`: specifies the host to be contacted.

Request Header Parameters In addition to the generic header parameters, the following headers are commonly used in the request that is sent to the API:

- `User-Agent`: identifies the client (= agent).

- `Referer`: specifies the URL from which the URL of the current request was obtained. This makes a lot of sense for HATEOAS based architectures.

- `Expect`: status code expected by the client.

- `From`: an email address of the end user sending the request.

- `Max-Forwards`: maximum number of hops in a TRACE request.

- `Accept`: specifies a list of media-types, which the user agent can accept as a response.

- `Accept-Charset`: specifies character sets, which the user agent can accept as a response.

- `Accept-Encoding`: specifies the encoding, which the user agent can accept as a response.

- `Accept-Language`: specifies the languages, which the user agent can accept as a response.

- `MIME-Version`: specifies the version of the MIME protocol that is used.

- `If-Match`: used for conditional HTTP requests, often in combination with caching (see section 11.3.1.2). The header value contains a hash code to indicate the version of the representation.

- `If-None-Match`: used for conditional HTTP requests, often in combination with caching (see section 11.3.1.2). The header value contains a hash code to indicate the version of the representation.

- `If-Modified-Since`: used for conditional HTTP requests, often in combination with caching (see section 11.3.1.2). The header value contains a timestamp to indicate the version of the representation.

- `If-Unmodified-Since`: used for conditional HTTP requests in combination with caching (see section 11.3.1.2). The header value contains a timestamp to indicate the version of the representation.

- `If-Range`: used for conditional HTTP requests, value for this header contains a condition, instructs the server to ignore the range header if the condition does not evaluate to true.

- `Authorization`: specifies authorization credentials.

- `Proxy-Authorization`: specifies authorization credentials for the proxy.

- `Pragma`: used for controlling the cache in HTTP 1.0, now replaced by the `Cache-Control` header.

Response Header Parameters In addition to the general header parameters, the following headers are commonly used in the response that is sent from the API to the clients:

- `Status`: HTTP status code, indicating success or the reason for failure.

267

- **Retry-After**: indicates how long the user agent should wait before retrying the request. Typically used in combination with 5xx status codes.

- **Location**: specifies the URL of a resource, which is relevant for this response, e.g. the URL of a recently created resource (with a 201 Created status code) or the URL to redirect to (with a 3xx status code).

- **Allow**: lists all the methods that can be used with the respective resource.

- **Server**: Just as the **User-Agent** header identifies the software that was used to produce the request, the **Server** header identifies the software and version that was used to produce the response. It can be used to analyze interoperability problems.

- **Vary**: indicates which request headers influence the selection of the representation during content negotiation.

- **Age**: indicates the amount of time that has passed since the response was generated.

- The **Cache-Control** header field is set by the API and is the main control for caching. It allows setting several directives:

    - The **max-age** {value} directive indicates that caches can hold cached values for max-age seconds. Example: **Cache-Control: max-age=3600**

    - The **no-cache** directive or no-store directive indicates that no caching should be performed on this resources. Example: **Cache-Control: no-cache**

    - The **public** directive indicates that no caching should be performed. Example: **Cache-Control: public**

- The `private` directive indicates that no caching should be performed. Example: `Cache-Control: private`
- The `must-revalidate` directive indicates that the server must be checked for each request. Example: `Cache-Control: must-revalidate`

- The `Date` header field is set by the API and indicates when the response was sent and helps clients to compute the refresh time.

- The `Last-Modified` header field is set by the API and indicates when the resource was last changed and helps clients to determine the freshness of the cached data.

- The `ETag` header field is set by the API and is a hash of the content and thus changes when the content changes. It can be used by clients to determine the freshness of the cached data.

- The `Expires` header field is set by the API and indicates the date at which the cached value expires. It is only used for backward compatibility with HTTP 1.0. In HTTP 1.1 it is replaced by the `Date` and `Cache-Control: max-age` header fields.

- `Warning`: It carries additional information about the status of a message. It is typically used to warn about cache inconsistencies.

- `Content-Range`: used when serving partial data of a representation. Specifies the range of the data that is included in this document.

- `WWW-Authenticate`: describes the authentication challenge. The header is typically sent in combination with a `401 Unauthorized` status code.

- **Proxy-Authenticate**: describes the authentication challenge. The header is typically sent in combination with a `407 Proxy Authentication Required` status code.

E. HTTP Status Codes

List of HTTP status codes:

- 100 `Continue`: indicates that the initial part of a request has been received.

- 101 `Switching Protocols`: indicates that the server is willing to comply with the client's request to change the protocol.

- 200 `OK`: indicates that the request has succeeded.

- 201 `Created`: indicates that one or more new resources have been created.

- 202 `Accepted`: indicates that the request has been accepted for processing but processing has not finished, yet.

- 203 `Non-Authoritative Information`: indicates that the request succeeded, but that the payload has been modified by a proxy. This status code is used by a proxy.

- 204 `No Content`: indicates that the request was successful but the HTTP body does not contain a response.

- 205 `Reset Content`: indicates that the request was successful and that the client needs to reset the sent data. It is typically applied when the user has entered data in a form, sent the request and in response the server indicates that the form shall be cleared (205 `Reset Content`) for entry of the next data set.

271

- 300 `Multiple Choices`: indicates that several resources are available as matching choices for the request.

- 301 `Moved Permanently`: Redirect to the address in the `Location` header. The new address is a permanent condition.

- 302 `Moved Temporarily`: Redirect to the address in the `Location` header. The new address is only a temporary condition.

- 303 `See Other`: Redirect to the address in the `Location` header, changing the HTTP method to GET.

- 307 `Temporary Redirect`: Redirect to the address in the `Location` header, preserving the original HTTP method.

- 400 `Bad Request`: The request is syntactically incorrect. For example: the request contains query parameters that cannot be processed.

- 401 `Unauthorized`: Request failed because the user is not authenticated in the first place.

- 402 `Insufficient Funds`: This happens for monetized APIs. The request failed because the authenticated user does not have sufficient funds, or a sufficiently large API plan.

- 403 `Forbidden`: The request failed for an authenticated user, who does not have authorization to access the requested resource.

- 404 `Not Found`: The requested resource is not found, e.g. a non-existing resource-id was specified as path parameter.

- **405 Method Not Allowed**: The HTTP method specified in the request is not allowed. The API needs to return a list of supported HTTP methods in the `Allow` header.

- **406 Not Acceptable**: The API cannot produce a response in any of the media-types that the client can accept.

- **408 Request Timeout**: indicates that the server did not receive a complete request.

- **409 Conflict**: indicates a conflict with the current state of the resource.

- **410 Gone**: indicates that the resource is no longer available.

- **411 Length Required**: The HTTP header `Content-Length` was not received; it needs to be sent by the client.

- **412 Precondition Failed**: indicates that the cache is stale.

- **413 Payload Too Large**: indicates that the payload is larger than the server can process.

- **414 URI Too Long**: indicates that the URI is too long. The root cause might be an attack, an improperly translated POST to GET or a broken, recursive redirection loop.

- **415 Unsupported Media Type**: indicates that the input sent in the HTTP body of the request is not in a format that can be processed by the server.

- **417 Expectation Failed**: The expectation that was sent in the `Expect` header by the client could not be fulfilled by the server.

- **422 Unprocessable Entity**: The HTTP body is semantically wrong, even though it is in the appropriate content-type and is syntactically correct.

- **426 Upgrade Required**: The server does not process the request, until the client upgrades to a later version of the protocol. The supported protocol versions are included in the `Upgrade` header of the response.

- **428 Precondition Required**: To prevent lost updates, the API may require a conditional HTTP request with either `If-Match`, `If-None-Match`, `If-Unmodified-Since` or `If-Modified-Since` header. If none is present, the API refuses to perform any writing access and sends this status code, as specified in IETF RFC 6585 [28].

- **500 Internal Server Error**: Some unexpected condition occurred in the API, e.g. an exception was thrown.

- **501 Not Implemented**: The functionality requested by the client is not implemented yet.

- **502 Bad Gateway**: The server acted as a gateway or proxy and got an invalid response from a backend.

- **503 Service Unavailable**: The server cannot fulfill the request or may refuse the connection. The reason is temporary overload or a scheduled maintenance.

- **504 Gateway Timeout**: The server acted as a gateway or proxy and got a timeout while waiting for the response from a backend.

- **505 HTTP Version Not Supported**: The server does not support the major HTTP version.

Bibliography

[1] Tim Berners-Lee. Hypertext style: Cool URIs don't change. Technical report, W3C, 1998. 7.2.4

[2] Matthias Biehl. *API Architecture: The Big Picture for Building APIs (API University Series) (Volume 2)*. CreateSpace Independent Publishing Platform, 1 edition, May 2015. 1.5

[3] Matthias Biehl. *OAuth 2.0: Getting Started in Web-API Security (API University Series) (Volume 1)*. CreateSpace Independent Publishing Platform, 1 edition, January 2015. 11.1.3.4, 11.1.4.4

[4] Nathaniel S. Borenstein and Ned Freed. Multipurpose internet mail extensions (MIME) part one: Format of internet message bodies. Technical Report 2045, RFC Editor, Fremont, CA, USA, November 1996. 7.3.2

[5] John Bradley, Nat Sakimura, and Michael Jones. JSON web signature (JWS). Technical Report 7515, RFC Editor, Fremont, CA, USA, May 2015. 11.1.3.5

[6] John Bradley, Nat Sakimura, and Michael Jones. JSON web token (JWT). Technical Report 7519, RFC Editor, Fremont, CA, USA, May 2015. 11.1.3.5

[7] T. Bray. The JavaScript object notation (JSON) data interchange format. Technical Report 7159, RFC Editor, Fremont, CA, USA, March 2014. 7.3.7

[8] Erik Christensen, Francisco Curbera, Greg Meredith, and Sanjiva Weerawarana. Web service definition language (WSDL). Technical report, March 2001. 4.3, 5.3.4

[9] James Clark and Steve DeRose. XML path language (XPath) version 1.0, 1999. 10.2.3

[10] Gary Court, Kris Zyp, and Francis Galiegue. JSON schema: core definitions and terminology. Technical Report draft-zyp-json-schema-04.txt, IETF Secretariat, Fremont, CA, USA, January 2013. 7.3.7.1, 8.4, 9.3

[11] Mark Davis and Addison Phillips. Tags for identifying languages. Technical Report 5646, RFC Editor, Fremont, CA, USA, September 2009. D

[12] Lisa Dusseault and James M. Snell. PATCH method for HTTP. Technical Report 5789, RFC Editor, Fremont, CA, USA, March 2010. 7.5.2.5

[13] Roy Fielding and Julian Reschke. Hypertext transfer protocol (HTTP/1.1): Authentication. Technical Report 7235, RFC Editor, Fremont, CA, USA, June 2014. 6.1, 11.1.3.2, 11.1.3.3

[14] Roy Fielding and Julian Reschke. Hypertext transfer protocol (HTTP/1.1): Conditional requests. Technical Report 7232, RFC Editor, Fremont, CA, USA, June 2014. 6.1, 7.6

[15] Roy Fielding and Julian Reschke. Hypertext transfer protocol (HTTP/1.1): Message syntax and routing. Technical Report 7230, RFC Editor, Fremont, CA, USA, June 2014. 6.1

[16] Roy Fielding and Julian Reschke. Hypertext transfer protocol (HTTP/1.1): Semantics and content. Technical Report

7231, RFC Editor, Fremont, CA, USA, June 2014. 6.1, 7.5.3

[17] Roy T. Fielding. *Architectural styles and the design of network-based software architectures*. PhD thesis, University of California, Irvine, Irvine - Irvine, CA 92697, USA, 2000. 6, 6.5

[18] Erich Gamma, Richard Helm, Ralph Johnson, and John Vlissides. *Design Patterns: Elements of Reusable Object-Oriented Software*. Addison-Wesley Professional, 1 edition, November 1994. 7.1.3

[19] Stefan Goessner. JSONPath - XPath for JSON, February 2007. 10.2.3

[20] JSON-RPC Working Group. JSON-RPC 2.0 specification. Technical report, 2013. 5.3.3.2

[21] Marc J. Hadley. Web application description language (WADL). Technical report, W3C, 2006. 4.3

[22] Dick Hardt. The OAuth 2.0 authorization framework. Technical Report 6749, RFC Editor, Fremont, CA, USA, October 2012. 11.1.3.4

[23] Joe Hildebrand and Michael Jones. JSON web encryption (JWE). Technical Report 7516, RFC Editor, Fremont, CA, USA, May 2015. 11.1.3.5

[24] IANA. MIME Media Types, March 2007. 7.3.2, 7.4.2.4, B

[25] John Klensin, Tony Hansen, and Ned Freed. Media type specifications and registration procedures. Technical Report 6838, RFC Editor, Fremont, CA, USA, January 2013. 7.3.2, 7.4.2.4, B

[26] Yves Lafon, Roy Fielding, and Julian Reschke. Hypertext transfer protocol (HTTP/1.1): Range requests. Technical Report 7233, RFC Editor, Fremont, CA, USA, June 2014. 6.1

[27] Larry Masinter, Tim Berners-Lee, and Roy T. Fielding. Uniform resource identifier (URI): Generic syntax. Technical Report 3986, RFC Editor, Fremont, CA, USA, January 2005. 7.2

[28] M. Nottingham and R. Fielding. RFC 6585 - additional HTTP status codes. Technical report, Internet Engineering Task Force (IETF), April 2012. 7.6, 11.3.3.3, 11.4.2.1, E

[29] Mark Nottingham. Web linking. Technical Report 5988, RFC Editor, Fremont, CA, USA, October 2010. 7.1.8, 11.2.3

[30] Mark Nottingham and Paul Bryan. JavaScript object notation (JSON) patch. Technical Report 6902, RFC Editor, Fremont, CA, USA, April 2013. 7.5.1.3, 7.5.2.5

[31] Mark Nottingham, Paul Bryan, and Kris Zyp. JavaScript object notation (JSON) pointer. Technical Report 6901, RFC Editor, Fremont, CA, USA, April 2013. 10.2.3

[32] Mark Nottingham, Roy Fielding, and Julian Reschke. Hypertext transfer protocol (HTTP/1.1): Caching. Technical Report 7234, RFC Editor, Fremont, CA, USA, June 2014. 6.1

[33] Mark Nottingham and Erik Wilde. Problem details for HTTP APIs. Technical Report 7807, RFC Editor, Fremont, CA, USA. 7.6.3.3

[34] N. Sakimura, J. Bradley, M. Jones, B. de Medeiros, and C. Mortimore. OpenID connect core 1.0. Technical report, November 2014. 11.1.3.5

[35] J. Snell and P. Hoffman. JSON merge patch. Technical Report 7396, RFC Editor, Fremont, CA, USA, October 2014. 7.5.1.3, 7.5.2.5, B

[36] Simon S. St. Laurent, Joe Johnston, and Edd Dumbill. *Programming Web Services with XML-RPC*. O'Reilly & Associates, Sebastopol, CA, 2001. 5.3.3.3

[37] Anne van Kesteren. Cross-Origin resource sharing. Technical report, W3C. 7.9.1

[38] W3C. XSL transformations (XSLT). Technical report, W3C, November 1999. 10.2.3

[39] W3C. Simple object access protocol (SOAP) 1.2. Technical report, W3C, April 2007. 5.3.4

Index

A
Accept, 126, 141, 239, 266
Acceptance Tests, 49
Accept-Charset, 127, 266
Accepted, 106, 271
Accept-Encoding, 127, 266
Accept-Language, 126, 266
Access-Control-Allow-Origin, 166
Age, 268
Agile, 38
AJAX, 165
Allow, 142, 157, 268, 273
API, 92
API Consumers, 30
API Description Language, 57, 169, 183
API Keys, 208
API Prototype, 44, 47
API Skeleton, 63
Application State, 95
Approachable, 73
Architectural Patterns, 75
Architectural Styles, 79
Asynchronous JavaScript and XML, 165
Attacks, 208
Authentication, 207
Authorization, 137, 141, 207, 267
Authorization Header, 210
Automatic Discovery, 249
Availability, 74

B
Backend Errors, 202
Backward Compatible Changes, 236
Bad Gateway, 274
Bad Request, 157, 272

C
Cache-Control, 228, 268
Cache-Control: max-age, 228, 268
Cache-Control: must-revalidate, 228, 269
Cache-Control: no-cache, 228, 268
Cache-Control: private, 228, 269

Cache-Control: public, 228, 268
Caching, 222
camelCase, 130
Challenge-Response, 210
Changes, Backward Compatible, 236
Changes, Incompatible, 237
Clean, 72
Clear, 73
Client, 63, 243
Client Error, 157
Client Server Patterns, 75
Client Stub, 63
Code Generation, 63
Code Injection, 216
Collection Resources, 105
Compatible, 73
Compliant, 74
Conditional DELETE, 227
Conditional GE, 226
Conditional GET, 226
Conditional PUT, 227
Conflict, 273
CONNECT, 263
Consistency, 162
Consumer Discovery, 248
Consumer-Centric, 72
Consumer-Oriented, 29
Consumers, 30
Content Negotiation, 124
Content-Encoding, 265
Content-Language, 265
Content-Length, 265

Content-Location, 265
Content-MD5, 265
Content-Range, 269
Content-Type, 122, 139, 140, 157, 265
Continue, 271
Contract Negotiation, 61
Contract-First Design, 37
Contract-first Design, 61
Controller Resources, 106
CORS, 165
Created, 271
Cross-Origin Resource Sharing, 165
Cross-Site Request Forgery, 165
Cross-Site Scripting, 165
CRUD, 90, 92, 143
CSRF, 165
Customer Experience, 25
Customer Focus, 25

D

Data Structure Transformation, 198
Date, 229, 265, 269
Delegation, 207
DELETE, 146, 149, 263
Demo App, 45
Denial of Service Attacks, 230
Design Contract, 61
Design Repository, 61
Design Thinking, 33
Design-time Discovery, 248

Developer Experience, 25, 31, 101
Discoverable, 73
Discovery, 63, 167, 248
Domain Specific Languages, 60
DOS, 230
DSL, 60
DX, 101

E
Entity Tag, 225
Error Handling, 156
Error Message, 159
ETag, 225, 229, 269
Evolution, 235
Expect, 266
Expectation Failed, 273
Expires, 229, 269
Explorable, 73

F
Facade Pattern, 77
Forbidden, 158, 272
Forgiving, 73
Form Parameters, 139
FREAK, 215
From, 266

G
Gateway Timeout, 274
GET, 147, 148, 263
Gone, 273
Green Field Approach, 195

H
HATEOAS, 98
HATEOAS Style, 80
HEAD, 147, 151, 263
Header Parameters, 139
Host, 265
HTTP, 89
HTTP Basic, 209
HTTP Digest, 210
HTTP Header Fields, 139
HTTP Headers, 139
HTTP Status Code, 153
HTTP Version Not Supported, 274
Hypertext Transfer Protocol, 89

I
ID Token, 213
Idempotent, 92, 153
Identity, 208
If-Match, 266
If-Modified-Since, 267
If-None-Match, 267
If-Range, 267
If-Unmodified-Since, 226, 267
Incompatible Changes, 237
Input Validation, 216
Inside-out, 36
Instance Resources, 104
Insufficient Funds, 158, 272
Integrity, 208
Interactive Documentation, 61

283

Internal Server Error, 159, 274
Interoperable, 72
Intuitive, 73
Intuitive Use, 162
IP-Restriction, 214

J

JavaScript Object Notation, 129
JSON, 129
JSON Anti Patterns, 131
JSON Path, 202
JSON Pointer, 202
JSON Schema, 66, 130, 175, 216
JSON Schemas, 186
JSONP, 132
JSON-RPC, 81
JWT, 201, 213

L

Last-Modified, 226, 229, 269
Legacy Approach, 195
Length Required, 273
Location, 142, 156, 241, 268, 272
Logging, 204
Logs, 52

M

Max-Forwards, 266
Media-Type, 140, 265
Method Not Allowed, 157, 273
Metrics, 52

MIME-Type, 140, 265
MIME-Version, 266
Moved Permanently, 156, 272
Moved Temporarily, 156, 272
Multiple Choices, 272

N

Negative Caching, 223
No Content, 271
Non-Authoritative Information, 271
Not Acceptable, 157, 273
Not Found, 157, 272
Not Implemented, 159, 274

O

OAuth, 212, 258
OK, 271
OpenAPI, 169
OpenID Connect, 213, 259
Optimistic Rate Limitation, 233
OPTIONS, 147, 151, 167, 263
Output Validation, 216
Outside-in, 36

P

Pagination, 220
PascalCase, 130
PATCH, 146, 150, 263
Path Parameters, 138
Payload Too Large, 273
Performance, 74
Pilot Consumers, 49
POODLE, 215

POST, 144, 148, 263
Pragma, 267
Pragmatic REST, 84
Precondition Failed, 273
Precondition Required, 227, 274
Predictable, 73
Products, 25, 29
Prototypical API Consumer, 33
Prototyping, 47
Proxy Pattern, 78
Proxy-Authenticate, 270
Proxy-Authorization, 267
PUT, 145, 149, 263

Q
Query Parameters, 138
Quota, 234

R
RAML, 183
Rate Limitation, 231
Redirection, 155
Referer, 266
Reports, 52
Representation, 90, 92
Representation Transformation, 199
Representational State Transfer, 89
Representations, 121
Request Header Parameters, 141, 266
Request ID, 204
Request Timeout, 273
Request Transformation, 197
Request-URI Too Long, 120
Requirements Engineering, 33
Reset Content, 271
Resource, 90, 91
Resource State, 95
Resources, 102
Response Header Parameters, 141
Response Transformation, 198
REST, 89, 91
REST Style, 79
RESTful, 89
Retry-After, 142, 158, 268
Reusable, 29, 74
Richardson Maturity Model, 84
Robustness, 167
Root Resource, 107
RPC Style, 81
Runtime Discovery, 249

S
Safe, 93, 153
SAML, 201
SAML2 Bearer Profile, 259
Sanitizing, 204
Scalable, 74
Secure, 74
Security, 205
Security Concerns, 207
Security Mechanisms, 208

Security Mediation, 201
See Other, 106, 156, 272
Self-Explanatory, 73
Server, 142, 268
Server Error, 158
Service Unavailable, 159, 274
Simple, 72
Simulation, 64
Simulations, 38
Single Source of Truth, 58
SLAs, 230
snake_case, 130
SOAP Style, 82
Spike Limitation, 233
Spike Smoothing, 233
SQL Injection, 216
Standards, 72
State, 94
Stateful Server Pattern, 76
Stateless Server Pattern, 76
Status, 141, 267
Status Code, 153
Sub Resource, 108
Swagger, 169
Switching Protocols, 271

T

Temporary Redirect, 156, 272
Time-Restriction, 214
TLS, 214
Too Many Requests, 158, 232, 233
TRACE, 147, 151, 263
Tracking ID, 204

Traffic Bursts, 233
Traffic Shaping, 230
Traffic Spikes, 233
Transaction ID, 204
Transformation Tools, 201
Transport Layer Security, 214

U

UDDI, 249
Unauthorized, 158, 210, 272
Uniform HTTP Interface, 90
Uniform Resource Identifier, 90
Uniform Resource Interface, 92, 142
Uniform Resource Locator, 90
Uniform Resource Name, 90
Unprocessable Entity, 158, 274
Unsupported Media Type, 157, 273
Upgrade Required, 274
URI, 90
URI Too Long, 273
URL, 90
URN, 90
User Experience, 101
User-Agent, 141, 266
UX, 101

V

Validation, 215
Vary, 126, 268
Version, Major, 239
Version, Minor, 239

Versioning, 235, 239
Visibility, 86, 98

W
Warning, 269
Web Service Description Language, 82
WebSockets, 83
Well-Documented, 73
WSDL, 82, 249
WWW-Authenticate, 269
WWW-Authenticate: Basic, 210

X
X.509, 214
XML Schemas, 186
XML-RPC, 81
XMPP, 83
XPath, 202
XRateLimitLimit, 232
XRateLimitRemaining, 232
XRateLimitReset, 232
XSLT, 201
XSS, 165

Y
YAML, 183

Made in the USA
Columbia, SC
19 March 2018